The Clifton–Morenci Strike

THE CLIFTON-MORENCI STRIKE
Labor Difficulty in Arizona, 1915-1916

James R. Kluger

THE UNIVERSITY OF ARIZONA PRESS
Tucson, Arizona

About the Author . . .

JAMES ROBERT KLUGER received his B.A. from St. Ambrose College in 1961, then earned an M.A. in history from the University of Arizona in 1965. He taught at Midwestern College in Denison, Iowa, and in 1967 returned to the University of Arizona to begin work on his Ph.D. in Recent and Western History. He is the title-page editor's assistant for the Western History Association on the University of Arizona Press book *Reflections of Western Historians.* In 1969 he was awarded the John P. Rockfellow Memorial Scholarship for excellence in Western History.

The University of Arizona Press
www.uapress.arizona.edu

Printed in the United States of America
21 20 19 18 17 16   7 6 5 4 3 2

ISBN-13: 978-0-8165-0267-7 (cloth)
ISBN-13: 978-0-8165-3529-3 (Century Collection paper)

L. C. No. 72-116692

♾ This paper meets the requirements of ANSI/NISO Z39.48-1992
(Permanence of Paper).

For my nephews
Kevin and Gregory

Contents

Foreword

Very little has been written about the history of labor-management relations in Arizona's copper mining districts. This is due primarily to the attraction of more exciting subjects, such as the Indian wars, a certain reluctance to probe disagreeable aspects of Arizona's recent past, and a general lack of access to company and union records. Of the labor history that has appeared, much of it has focused on the sensationalism surrounding the wartime deportations of militant workers from Jerome and Bisbee during the summer of 1917. However, there is another side, a positive side, to Arizona's labor history. Whereas walkouts in most other Western states and territories were characterized by clashes with strikebreakers, property destruction, and physical violence and deaths, all of these were noticeably lacking in Arizona's labor difficulties. Perhaps the best example of this can be seen in the strike that paralyzed the mining camps of Clifton and Morenci during the early winter of 1915, which James Kluger ably describes and analyzes on the succeeding pages.

The Clifton-Morenci district was the first major copper producer in Arizona. Located in southeastern Arizona, in the precipitous mountains near the junction of the San Francisco River and Chase Creek, this district was developed in the mid-1870s by Charles and Henry Lesinsky, Silver City, New Mexico, merchants, who imported Mexican labor to construct buildings, erect a crude smelter, and begin mining operations. The processed copper ore was hauled by wagon overland to the railhead in Colorado. To promote stability in the community, the operators tried to employ married men who would bring their families to Clifton. In 1882 the Lesinskys sold out to Arizona Copper Company, Limited, a Scotch concern, which modernized the operations at Clifton and built a railroad from Lordsburg. At nearby Morenci, the Detroit Copper Company opened additional mines and established a camp. The early 1890s brought hard times, but by the close of the decade prosperity had returned.

Although representatives of labor unions were entering the Arizona copper camps by 1900, most of their efforts were concentrated in the interior districts. In Globe-Miami, Bisbee, and Jerome, particularly, the American Federation of Labor (A.F. of L.) attempted to organize the crafts, while the Western Federation of Miners (W.F. of M.) sought to form locals among the unskilled workers. They attained some success in 1903 when the territorial legislature passed an eight-hour law, and mine operators in unionized districts reduced the work shifts accordingly without lowering wages. At Clifton-Morenci, however, where there were no union locals, the act was circumvented, and a strike ensued. Management blamed outside agitators for the trouble, and, fearing violence from the predominantly Mexican labor force, called for help. A devastating flash flood, coupled with the arrival of the National Guard, federal troops, and Arizona Rangers, quickly ended the worst strike before statehood.

During the following decade organized labor accomplished very little in Arizona. With nine chartered locals, the Western Federation in 1907 called a strike at Bisbee to protest the layoff of some of its members, but the companies hired non-union workers, and the men gave up several months later. At Clifton-Morenci smelter workers walked off their jobs because of wage cuts, seriously curtailing production, but soon returned to work without realizing any gains. A primary reason for the organization's weakness was the internal dissension within the W.F. of M. throughout the West. The bickering was caused by a militant, left-wing element which in 1905 joined with other radical groups to form the Industrial Workers of the World (I.W.W.) and then began seeking control of the W.F. of M. locals. Unable to present a solid front, union activity in Arizona languished for several years.

In 1915 there was a resurgence of labor in Arizona, caused by the depression which began in 1914. In January the A.F. of L. affiliates at Globe-Miami, protesting a ten percent wage cut, called a strike which spread throughout the district. W.F. of M. and I.W.W. locals joined the walkout. As the operators refused to deal with the workers through any union organization, Governor George W. P. Hunt, who had strong labor support, went to the scene and opened negotiations. Management agreed to restore the wage cuts for the crafts and institute a sliding pay scale based on copper prices for the miners. The Miami scale was soon regarded as the best in the state.

During the late summer, the miners at Clifton-Morenci invited a W.F. of M. organizer into their district. They desired higher wages and an end to oppressive actions by company officials. In mid-September almost five thousand men went on strike. The mine operators flatly refused to meet with W. F. of M. representatives, but carefully avoided inciting the workers; the strike organizers maintained constant vigilance to keep their followers in line. The walkout gained nationwide attention. Nearly five months later, in January of 1916, after both state and federal mediators had intervened, an agreement finally was reached. The companies consented to a wage increase and an adjustment of other grievances; the miners agreed to abandon the W.F. of M. and join an A.F. of L. affiliate.

This strike occurred at a crucial time in Western labor history. The activities of the W.F. of M. leaders in Clifton-Morenci and elsewhere convinced many of its members that the organization had become impotent, and they launched a movement within its ranks to revitalize the union. At its national convention held in Great Falls, Montana, in July of 1916, the W.F. of M. voted to seek a new identification completely apart from the radical I.W.W. by changing its name to the International Union of Mine Mill and Smelter Workers. During World War I the Mine-Mill Workers saw their locals infiltrated by I.W.W. agitators, but the return of peace brought an end to radicalism and a more optimistic future.

James Kluger's excellent study of the Clifton-Morenci Strike of 1915–16 is an important addition to the industrial history of Arizona. It emphasizes that the state's early labor-management relations were remarkably free of the radicalism, violence, and industrial strife that swept other Rocky Mountain mining camps. It also provides insight into feelings concerning ethnic groups, the fears of management regarding unionism, and labor's crude approach to making itself heard during these years. And, coming at a time when Western labor was purging itself of radicalism and recharting its goals, the Clifton-Morenci strike may well have been a milestone in organized labor's groping for recognition in the West.

HARWOOD P. HINTON
Editor, Arizona and the West

Preface

The Clifton-Morenci strike of 1915–16 in Arizona is one of thousands of incidents in our past that has had its hour upon the national stage and then is heard of no more; the ripple of recognition recedes into the stream of history. But this strike, and so many like it, was an important part of the American labor movement, an inclusive term usually associated with Homestead, Haymarket, and a host of other dramatic clashes between unions and management.

Violence did not erupt in Arizona in 1915. This notable absence of bloodshed makes the Clifton-Morenci strike unique in that time of industrial turbulence and poses the question of who deserves credit, rather than who is to blame, for the nature of the walkout. It allows us to view more lightly the incidents that in a sanguinary situation might have led to disaster. Finally, it illustrates the basic antagonism inherent when two forces clash over a principle — in this case, union recognition.

During this period, Arizona officials were taunted for many of their progressive innovations, and Governor George W. P. Hunt was castigated on numerous occasions for his activities by both state and national newspapers. The Western Federation of Miners constantly was under attack by a hostile press for its operations. The strike in Clifton and Morenci did not escape journalistic scrutiny or condemnation. Yet for all the critical comments and dire predictions, the walkout remained peaceful and ended without the adverse consequences so many had foreseen.

In writing this book, I am first of all indebted to my friend and teacher John Alexander Carroll, in whose seminar this study was begun, and under whom it was completed as my master's thesis at the University of Arizona in 1965. Whatever I know about writing history I owe to him. To Dr. Harwood P. Hinton, who next became my adviser, I am most grateful for aid and encouragement, both in revising this manuscript for publication and in my graduate program. I also thank him for graciously consenting to write the foreword to this book.

It was a pleasure to have the opportunity to work with Marshall Townsend and the other staff members of the University of Arizona Press. Mrs. Karen Thure was of particular assistance. Her cheerful demeanor was coupled with a perceptive editorial eye. I also want to thank Charles C. Colley and Margaret Sparks of the Arizona Pioneers' Historical Society for providing the illustrations. Chuck Colley also drew the excellent map that graces the book. Finally, to my parents I owe a very special debt of gratitude — for everything.

JAMES R. KLUGER

The Clifton-Morenci Strike

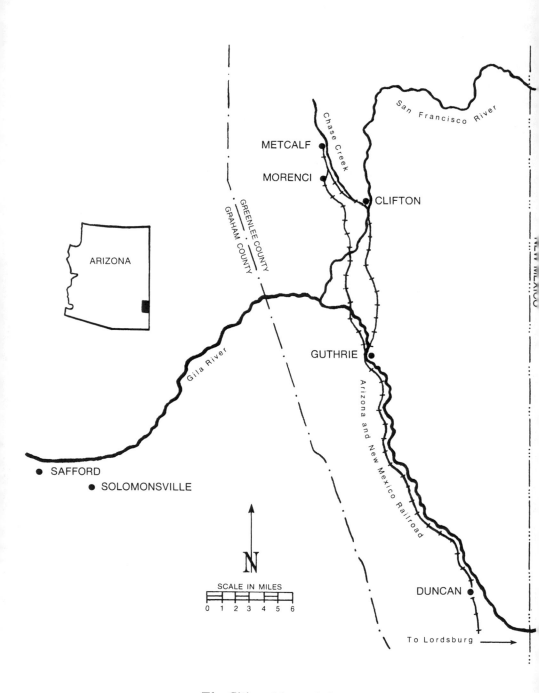

The Clifton-Morenci Area

CHAPTER 1

Background of the Strike

It was almost 11 o'clock on Saturday night, September 11, 1915. Soon replacements would come and the tired miners would be finished for another shift. Sunday would mean church and rest for some of the men, just rest for others. Eight hours earlier, when they entered the musty shafts of the Detroit Copper Company mine, the Clifton-Morenci district was alive with rumors and speculation of a strike, but the men had soon forgotten such talk as they went about their arduous and monotonous tasks. Suddenly they heard shouts: "Get out!" "We're on strike!" Most of the workers, electrified by the cries, left their tools and mules, rushed through the adits into the crisp night air, and joined the howling mob outside. Pickets were thrown up around the mine entrances, smelters, and concentrators, while bands of men fanned out through the tunnels, ejecting reluctant workers. The miners loitered about for a while, but gradually the crowd dissipated as small groups, discussing the day's events and anticipating tomorrow's, drifted off toward their shanties and sleep.[1]

The next morning, union organizers ordered employees of the Arizona Copper Company and the Shannon Copper Company to cease work, and at two o'clock that same day the smelters of these companies were shut down. Tap matter was left in the furnaces, and the charges in the converters were not blown. Almost five thousand workers were idle. Power for lighting purposes and the daily train were the only signs of industrial life in the entire district. The power plants which supplied electricity to the area had been seized by the strikers on Sunday and shut down for three nights. Service was restored on Wednesday, however, after Sheriff James G. Cash persuaded the miners to surrender the facilities and convinced company officials to reopen them under the protection of his office. The train to Clifton and Morenci was not interfered with because, as one striker put it, "That's our bean wagon." [2]

The Clifton-Morenci copper mining district, located in Greenlee County in southeastern Arizona near the New Mexico border, was an isolated community in 1915. Clifton, with its numerous "suburbs," had about ten thousand residents, and was the county seat. Strung out on both sides of the San Francisco River about five miles northwest of the confluence of that stream with the Gila, the town was a hodgepodge of streets and buildings erected wherever there was room to build. [3]

Two miles up Chase Creek, which flowed into the San Francisco near the heart of Clifton, a road "as wide and as smooth as a boulevard" led five miles west through Morenci Canyon to Morenci, which had a population of about eight thousand. In the climb from Clifton, the altitude rose from 3,466 feet to 5,000 feet. Metcalf, a community of one thousand inhabitants, was seven miles almost straight north up Chase Creek from Clifton. To enter the district, a visitor could take either the road from Duncan or Solomonville, or he could travel by rail from Lordsburg, New Mexico, through Guthrie, into the area. [4]

During the first two decades of the 20th century, three copper companies — the Arizona Copper Company, the Detroit Copper Mining Company, and the Shannon Consolidated Copper Company — maintained an industrial "barony" in the district. The Arizona Copper Company Ltd. had been hastily organized in Edinburgh, Scotland, on March 9, 1883, in order to buy the Longfellow Mining Company. Robert Metcalf, for whom Metcalf was named, staked the original claims to the Longfellow property and sold them to Charles and Henry Lesinsky in 1872. The Lesinskys in turn sold them to Frank L. Underwood in September 1882, for $1,500,000. Underwood sold the property to the Scotch interests six months later for $2,000,000. Clifton was the main domain of this Scottish firm. [5]

The Detroit Copper Mining Company held sway in Morenci. It had been founded in 1875 in Detroit, with E. B. Ward as the principal stock-

*The Detroit Copper Mining Company store
in Morenci at the time of the strike.*

holder. William Church, founder of Morenci, bought Ward's controlling interests in 1880 and began to develop the claims. In need of financial assistance, Church approached the Phelps Dodge Company. Although their principal business was exporting cotton to England and importing tin and other metals to the United States, they advanced him the money. In 1897 Phelps Dodge purchased the Detroit Company.[6]

The Shannon Copper Company, the smallest member of the three, was largely in the hands of Boston financiers and had Metcalf for its "sphere of influence." It had been organized in 1901.[7]

More than just employers, these three companies controlled almost every aspect of the workers' lives. Merchandise was brought into the district on the railroad owned by the Arizona Company and sold in company stores — the Arizona Copper Company Store Department in Clifton or the Phelps Dodge Mercantile Store in Morenci. Men lived in either company-owned houses, or in houses built on company property. These homes were lighted by company power plants and furnished with water from company reservoirs. Long before Arizona adopted prohibition in 1914, saloons were forbidden in Morenci. One could purchase beer and light wine by the pint at the company store, but only at certain times.[8]

Such subsidiary enterprises of the mining corporations were a special source of irritation to the workers. In 1917 Charles F. Willis, director of the Arizona State Bureau of Mines, pointed out four major problems which had caused an upswing in the number of strikes in Arizona after the start of World War I. These included too much leisure time to become dissatisfied with one's way of life; the growing bigness of business with an attendant decline in loyalty to employers; indignation at company profits, especially in camps where many foreigners worked and the disparities of wealth were more acute; and bitter criticism of the nonproduction enterprises of companies. The men resented these latter endeavors, even when they operated at a reasonable basis of profit or when they provided things better than the men could furnish by themselves.[9]

In spite of the existence of some private businesses in the Clifton-Morenci district, over 80 percent of the workers were constantly in debt to their employers because of trading with the mercantile departments, either at the "urging" of the company or because credit was easy to obtain. Moreover, independent merchants were in no position to undersell the company stores. They existed at the pleasure of the town-owners, and were dependent upon the Arizona Company railroad to bring supplies to Clifton. Furthermore, few people would complain about being "forced" to make a bigger profit.[10]

Workers claimed that store managers were instructed to make from 50 to 200 percent profit on commodities, but the Phelps Dodge Mercan-

The mining towns circa 1915. Above: view of Clifton showing the San Francisco River. Below: Longfellow Hill in Morenci.

tile Department actually showed only an 8.38 percent profit in 1914. The month the strike began, sugar was selling for 10¢ a pound in 100-pound lots; flour cost $1.50 for 26 pounds, pink beans were a dime a pound, a lead pencil was 15¢, and a shave cost a quarter. Prices for staple items averaged 25 percent higher than at Phoenix, and more than at Springerville, Arizona, where goods were freighted 85 miles by wagon.[11]

If a determined miner hated the company store enough, he could patronize an independent merchant, even though he might not save any money in doing so. With other services, however, it was a different story. The companies had a monopoly on water, whether liquid or solid. The rates for water caused considerable consternation among the workers. Each man paid a fixed amount, which was deducted from his salary. In the spring of 1915, the Arizona Corporation Commission conducted an investigation and ordered changes in the operations of the water companies. Prior to June 1, each single man paid $1.25 per month, the head of a family or household $2.00. Thereafter, bachelors were charged $1.00 per month, and the rates for married men were reduced to $1.60.[12]

In spite of the decrease, the miners continued to complain that the rates were too high. Ice cooled men's attitude toward the companies as much as it did their food. While workers were paying $1.00 per 100 pounds in Clifton, ice shipped on contract from Bisbee to Fort Huachuca sold at 25¢ per 100 pounds. The managers' answers to the water question were couched in vague terms and limited mainly to an objection that the money for water was not paid to the companies but to the water plants. They never mentioned ice prices. These irritations did not constitute major complaints, but they did add to the miners' animosity toward their employers.[13]

The company hospital was one of the principal grievances of the men, and one upon which they would vent some of their most vociferous complaints. The Arizona Company operated a hospital under the name "Clifton Benevolent Society." Before the enactment of the Arizona Workman's Compulsory Compensation Law in 1913, the society was also an insurance company. The men paid $1.00 a month hospital dues plus 50¢ for the insurance. When the compensation law became effective, the hospital directors merely raised the fees so that the workers paid the same amount: $1.50 for a single man, $2.00 for a married man and his family. What irritated the miners was the additional fee for the use of the facilities. Workers had to pay $1.00 a day board for any family member confined to the hospital. The men themselves paid this amount for certain illnesses. For injuries and other sicknesses, they received free care but only half their regular pay while laid up.[14]

These medical facilities, workers contended, were another profitable venture for the companies in which workers had no voice. Actually, the miners were supposed to have had elected representation on the directorate, but from the beginning few took any interest in it. Hospital officials filled the vacancies on their own, and the strikers were probably unaware that they even had a right to a voice on the hospital board until union organizers called it to their attention.[15]

Lack of interest in such affairs was not surprising in view of the peculiar makeup of the labor force in the district. When the camp first opened in the 1880s, Mexicans were the only workers obtainable. According to A. T. Thomson, assistant general manager of Phelps Dodge, this cheaper class of labor was sought thereafter because of the character, the formation, and the higher cost of extracting and treating ore from the mines in Clifton-Morenci. In later years, the operators hired hundreds of Yaqui Indians, who sought the mines of Arizona rather than taking their chances with either of the warring factions in their native Mexico. Americans, constituting about 30 percent of the employees, held most of the occupations of skill and subordinate positions of trust.[16]

The inarticulate Mexicans suffered silently the dishonest and often brutal yoke of many of these lesser officials. Often workers complained among themselves of being compelled by petty foremen to buy chances on worthless, or nearly worthless, items, but what they particularly resented was the bribery required by minor officials to get or keep a job. Shift bosses collected from $5 to $15 a month for such services. Many foremen "double shot the turn," that is, they built shacks with the money thus obtained and rented them to the miners for $10 a month. Lacking any effective organization or machinery for reaching the managers, a worker who protested such practices usually found himself discharged; and discharge meant banishment from the district — the companies would have nothing to do with such a worker.[17]

The bribes came out of an already meager salary, the lowest of any Arizona mining camp. The managers did not deny the lower pay, but justified it because of the class of worker and the smaller percentage-yield of the ore. A sliding scale based on the average selling price of copper per pound in the previous month determined wage rates. The quotations used in setting these standards appeared in the weekly *Engineering and Mining Journal*. The major mining camps in the state had a minimum scale of $3.50 per turn for miners, with the rate automatically changing as copper prices went up or down. In the Clifton-Morenci district, Mexican miners received $2.39 for a 7½-hour shift, while their American counterparts were paid $2.89. Rates for other occupations were in proportion; at the time the strike was called, for example, muckers earned $1.92

per day. Although quoted as shift pay, wages were actually figured on an hourly basis. When Arizona adopted the eight-hour law in 1903, the managers utilized this new system to avoid paying the men for the time it took to get from the collar of the shaft to the working level and back again.[18]

The policy of cheap wages for cheap labor netted the companies handsome dividends during this period. The earnings from mining, combined with big "turn shooting" ventures like the mercantile departments, meant huge profits for the stockholders in New York, Boston, and Edinburgh. In 1912 Phelps Dodge earned 23 percent on its capital of 45 million dollars and its principal property, the Detroit Company, paid a dividend of 146 percent on a capitalization of 1 million dollars that year. In 1913, Shannon Copper, reputed to be the weakest financially of the three companies, paid better than $1.50 per share, its stock listing at around 6½ points. Events in Europe soon caused a temporary halt in such earnings, then an unprecedented rise in returns. The lowly miner in an isolated camp in southeastern Arizona knew little of the happenings across the ocean, but he felt the results in his pocketbook.[19]

At the outbreak of hostilities in August 1914, virtually all shipments of copper to Europe ceased. The metal was listed as absolute contraband, and as such could be seized and confiscated under traditional international law by any of the belligerents. Germany had been purchasing huge quantities throughout the spring and summer, and the demand rose even higher after the war began, but with the British controlling the seas, those sales were cut off. Because the English market was glutted with copper that had been sold on consignment, it was several months before any quantities were needed by that country. This was a serious blow to the copper companies in the United States, which exported 65 percent of their annual production to Europe. Arizona accounted for over one third of the nation's output of the metal, and felt the effects of the ban immediately. For three months, from August 8 until November 7, the *Engineering and Mining Journal* ceased copper quotations because sales were so small. With the sudden drop in both demand and price, directors throughout the country took immediate steps to curtail production.[20]

In the Clifton-Morenci district, the general managers of the three companies adjusted their operations to meet conditions. J. W. Bennie of the Shannon Company closed his plant entirely, while Milton McLean of Detroit Copper and Norman Carmichael of Arizona Copper cut wages ten percent across the board and discontinued some facilities. This action lowered a laborer's pay per shift to $1.60, while a miner earned $2.44. The managers also reduced the number of hours each man worked in order to employ as many as they could while the hard times lasted, and they gave preference to married employees wherever possible. In October the mercantile departments of the companies announced a "profit-sharing plan" by which employees received a five percent rebate on purchases for the duration of the copper depression.[21]

Five months after the outbreak of war, Great Britain agreed to give United States ships comparative freedom from interference on the seas. She and her allies began to feel a renewed need for copper, and the situation in the industry improved rapidly. By January 23, 1915, the price of copper, which had dipped to a low of 11¢, had risen to 14¢ a pound, supposedly the minimum at which stockholders could receive a reasonable return on their investment.[22]

On February 5, Bennie of the Shannon Company announced the resumption of operations. At the same time, the mine managers issued pay standards based on a new sliding scale with top wages when copper sold at 15¢ and over. The immediate increases were modest: a laborer's pay rose from $1.60 to $1.64 per shift, while a miner's earnings went from $2.44 to $2.51. On February 20 the mercantile departments declared an end to "profit-sharing." The district, it appeared, had returned to normal.[23]

As the price of copper continued to rise, the managers hoped to balance out the depressed period with extra profits. The workers, lacking organization, had no effective way to obtain a substantial pay raise to balance their losses unless the companies granted a pay hike. Managers McLean, Bennie, and Carmichael interpreted their workers' silence as satisfaction. While in unionized camps at Bisbee and Miami pay scales went up 12¢ per shift when the price of copper rose a penny, the Clifton-Morenci standard lagged; raises averaged only 8¢ per shift. In June 1915, copper averaged 19.477¢ a pound. This pushed the July wage scale, which was based on the previous month's average price, to an all-time high. Mexican laborers earned $2.00 per shift, miners $2.96. Nevertheless, these record rates were far behind the rest of the Arizona camps.[24]

Years of petty abuses and misunderstandings, culminating in scanty salaries during prosperous periods, had made the miners susceptible to union agitation. The few feeble attempts at organizing a union in the past had been miserable failures because the men lacked the experience in successful negotiating and the financial independence to endure a long strike. Realizing these facts, a group of workers asked an organizer from the Western Federation of Miners (WF of M) to come to the district. The Western Federation of Miners was organized in Butte, Montana, in 1893, and was affiliated with the American Federation of Labor until

1897. It was briefly allied with the International Workers of the World (IWW) in 1905, but rejoined the AF of L in 1911. Before the birth of the IWW, the WF of M figured in some of the most dramatic and bloody strikes in the history of the American labor movement. Among the names associated with the organization were Coeur d'Alene, Cripple Creek, Leadville, and Telluride.[25]

It was ironic that the Western Federation should be invited to Clifton-Morenci. In 1914 Arizona voters passed by 25,017 to 14,323 an initiative measure which would have allowed companies in the state to employ no more than 20 percent aliens. Interestingly, the electorate of Greenlee County had approved the law, 1,210 to 640, even though the mining companies in the Clifton area employed almost the converse of the proposed statute. More important, the Western Federation had been a leading advocate of this so-called 80 percent law, which would have deprived jobs to almost all the workers it now proposed to organize.[26]

Guy E. Miller, a member of the executive board of the federation, entered the district early in August with an assistant, "a half-breed Mexican named Tribolet." Miller had received his "baptism" in industrial strife as president of the local at Telluride during the "labor wars" of 1904 and, although Colorado labor relations were among the most turbulent in the country, he was a leader in the fight against radical unionism. In spite of the many grievances he found in Clifton-Morenci, his first attempts nonetheless were characterized by a notable lack of success. Many of the men distrusted him and Tribolet; most workers feared reprisals from the companies. Small groups of men began to hold clandestine meetings at Newtown, a Morenci "suburb" outside of the mining district proper where most of the Mexican miners lived. The organizers took advantage of Spanish-American societies which provided health and burial benefits to members. They promised to extend these benefits by securing better wages and working conditions.[27]

As union strength grew, the agitators came out in the open, but they were still not received very well. At a meeting in Morenci the second week in August, men shouted to Miller, "We can't understand you, speak in Spanish!" He withdrew, and as Charpentier, another of the organizers, began to address the crowd, he was greeted with cries of ¡otro toro! (more bull!), and "Speak English, we can't understand you!" Two men, reported to be company "spotters," tried to break up a later meeting. They were severely manhandled and told to leave the district. Sheriff James G. Cash, who had worked for the Arizona Copper Company for six years prior to his election in 1914, warned the union men that he would permit no violence. At the same time he served notice on the non-union men that any interference on their part with anyone's right to free speech and meetings would also be prohibited.[28]

Company officials quickly learned of the presence of labor agitators in the area, and at first attempted to discredit the Western Federation. They feared the organization because of the sanguinary reputation it had earned in other strikes, and they wanted to prevent strong union development in the district.

From José Tibbets, a well-known Morenci miner who had moved to Ray, where the WF of M attempted to organize itself in July after a strike had begun, the managers received the following telegram and distributed it as a circular:

> Federation has no union here; only a few boys belonging to Miami local. These boys are disgusted with the way they have been treated and are going to quit the union and demand their money back. Do not pay any attention to Tribolet; he is no good and deceived us all. As soon as he gets you in trouble he will leave and probably take your money same as he did here.[29]

But union membership continued to grow. On August 16 it was fed by a salary cut resulting from a decline in the price of copper during the previous month. This cut dropped a laborer's pay from $2.00 to $1.92, a miner from $2.96 to $2.89. Two days later the managers, hoping to stem the tide, requested a conference with their Latin-American employees. When Guy Miller showed up, they refused to meet. Then certain workers began circulating a petition announcing their satisfaction with conditions and requesting that the camp not be unionized. When all these measures failed, the companies began discharging men who had joined the union or who refused to sign the petition.[30]

On September 6 Miller held a meeting in Library Plaza at Clifton, where he outlined his plans. These included the presentation of demands to the managers, time for consideration of the requests, and, if this failed, a strike. In case a walkout was deemed necessary, he advised the men to stock up on provisions, adding that if they ran out before the strike ended, the union would "perhaps" come to the rescue. When more workers were discharged for union activity, the leaders changed their plans and decided to act swiftly.[31]

On Saturday morning, September 11, the three mine managers each received letters requesting that they hold a conference with a committee of their employees and that Guy Miller be admitted to the conference. Milton McLean was in his office at the time. He replied that he would meet a delegation of employees at any time, but that he would have nothing to do with Guy Miller or the Western Federation of Miners. J. W. Bennie wired a similar answer the next morning from California. Norman Carmichael, also out of town, concurred with the other managers when he was contacted.[32]

After receiving the reply from McLean, the union committee met and decided to call a strike against the Detroit Company that night, and to hold off action against the other two companies pending answers from their managers. At a hurried conference, men made plans for a strike that had been coming for years. Miller had been in the district only a month when he called the strike. Like the assassin at Sarajevo, he was not the cause of the events that followed; he merely touched the match.

CHAPTER 2

Early Attempts at Settlement

At the time the strike was called, the Western Federation of Miners was in bad condition. It had never recovered from a long and costly strike in Michigan in 1913 and 1914. Heavy unemployment during the 1914 depression had cut membership rolls and weakened the influence of the organization still further. Adding to its difficulties was Butte Miners' Union, the main financial source of the federation, which was in revolt against the central committee.[1]

The workers in the Clifton-Morenci district were unaware that the organizers had ordered the walkout without the authorization of the executive board of the WF of M and with only the slimmest hope of more than token monetary support from the federation. Nevertheless, by the time the strike was called nearly all of the miners — heeding the advice of Guy Miller — had exhausted their credit for provisions at the company stores. Such supplies would last only a short time. The men would then have to make other arrangements for necessities, give up the strike, or force an early settlement with the companies.[2]

The managers of the companies had been so confident that their attempts to avert the establishment of the WF of M in the district had met with success that two of them were out of town when the strike began; the walkout caught them totally unprepared. Their problem suddenly became one of elimination rather than prevention. They could not let the men feel that their united efforts had won them any advantage. This was especially true of the Detroit Copper Company. Phelps Dodge operated larger properties elsewhere, and it was important that the tactics of its Morenci employees be discredited lest they be adopted at other mines. The managers took the position that the question of wages and other "minor grievances" had been interjected for popular effect. The central issue, they maintained, was whether "outside agitators" would dominate or whether it would be an open camp.[3]

On September 17 Bennie, McLean, and Carmichael reiterated their stand against the federation and repeated their willingness to meet with their employees directly. In a statement issued that day, they laid down certain preliminaries to any conference. They insisted that committees selected for this purpose be chosen "at such time, place, and in such manner that all our former employees, whether union or non-union, may have participated in that selection" so they would know that the group fairly represented all the workmen and was not sent as a delegation of the Western Federation. After representatives were thus chosen, the managers were to be given time to confirm that their instructions were carried out. Further, the men were required to pass "appropriate resolutions" or "duly authorize" the committees not to demand recognition of the WF of M either then or at any time, and to state their desire and agreement to return to work provided that any existing difficulties be adjusted. When the men complied with these conditions, the statement concluded, it would be a "pleasure to meet with the proposed committee for the purpose of discussion."[4]

The next day, while the companies were formally turning their property over to Sheriff Cash for protection, the men began taking the prescribed steps for a conference which they hoped would lead to the resumption of operations at those properties. In the afternoon the employees of the Arizona Copper Company met at the Princess Theatre in Clifton and named a committee to represent them in negotiations. Delegates from the Detroit and Shannon companies were chosen at Morenci Wednesday morning. All of the men selected belonged to the union and were employees of the companies, but none were officials of the WF of M. No resolutions or instructions were given to the delegates at either gathering.[5]

After the meeting at Morenci, Guy Miller addressed the crowd in the plaza. In his speech he emphasized that he never demanded anything of the managers. The word "demand," he said, did not belong in labor disputes because such disputes should be worked out by reason. Knowing that the federation would not be able to support the strike, the organizer told the men that he was willing to waive recognition "at this time" in order that industrial harmony might be quickly restored to the community. At Clifton later that day, he explained to the workers gathered in Library Plaza that recognition would require a long struggle and that he could not ask the men to pay such a price just then. He concluded, however, that he hoped "relations between employer and employee will be such that the managers will have no objection to my intervention when I may come again." [6]

When the managers were given the list of delegates, they asked if the workers had complied with the other provisions. Since the men had not passed any resolutions or given their representatives any instructions, the managers still refused to meet with them. On Thursday, September 23, Walter Douglas, general manager of Phelps Dodge, and Charles H. Moyer, president of the Western Federation, both arrived in the district. Douglas immediately went into conference with the managers, and Moyer met with the union leaders. [7]

The following day the strikers in Morenci passed a resolution waiving recognition of the federation and declaring their willingness to return to work "upon the adjustment of differences." That night workers in Clifton adopted the statement, and the following morning employees at Metcalf ratified the declaration. Moyer confidently predicted that the strike would be over in 48 hours. Unlike Miller, however, he saw nothing wrong with "demands," and listed three points which the workers would insist upon: a higher wage scale, reinstatement of men unjustly discharged since September 1, and assurances of no discrimination against the strike leaders. At eight o'clock the managers announced their willingness to meet the committee the following morning. [8]

An air of optimism pervaded Clifton Sunday morning. Somberly dressed Mexican women talked anxiously among themselves as they filed into church. While devout señoras prayed for an end to the strike, fidgety youngsters whispered and giggled. Mothers alternated between fervent petitions to Our Lady of Guadalupe and stern reprimands to their impish offspring.

Outside, men began congregating in small groups in the plaza, on the courthouse lawn, and in front of the offices of the Arizona Copper Company. They scrutinized each of the company officials as he entered the building. Each became the topic of conversation until he was replaced by the next arrival. A few minutes before eleven, the representatives of the strikers walked through the picket line and went into the building. For three hours the workers waited and watched. Shortly after two, the sober-faced strike committee reappeared, made a terse announcement that the managers would have a statement at four o'clock, and left for the union headquarters in Newtown. The men knew that the conference had been a failure; nevertheless, they waited for the official word.

The statement from the companies confirmed the suspicions of the strikers; the tone of the reply disheartened them. The managers contended that "agitators" of the Western Federation had entered the district, persuaded their former employees that the "past pleasant relations and present rate of wages should be radically changed," and called the strike without any presentation of grievances. In spite of the fact that large numbers of workers were willing to return to work, Bennie, McLean, and Carmichael felt that any attempt to recommence work would be to invite violence and intimidation. They were prepared to shut down indefinitely, they said, and arrogantly asserted:

> When it shall appear that conditions in this section warrant it and the companies are satisfied that the general sentiment of the community and their former employees is unanimously in favor of a resumption of operations on a basis of wages and conditions which have prevailed heretofore in this district, the companies reserve to themselves the right to decide as to whether or not they will again start up their plants.[9]

Although their main objection of union recognition had been waived by the strikers, company officials were concerned about the continued presence of federation organizers in the district. They apparently felt that the labor leaders would complicate the settlement of the "minor" issues, especially the wage question. The managers maintained that the Shannon and Detroit companies, which employed half of the workers in the area, could not continue to operate with any substantial increase in wages. They held that the demand for a $3.50 per day minimum for all underground miners was impossible with 13¢ copper, the base from which the proposed wage scale ascended. The question tended to be somewhat academic. Yearly copper prices actually had not been under 13¢ since 1911, and even in the depression year of 1914, the metal averaged 13.602¢ per pound. Furthermore, copper was selling at almost 18¢ in September 1915.[10]

E. W. Lewis, an attorney and spokesman for the Shannon Company, said that a wage increase, even if possible, would not benefit present employees, but would cause a substitution of Mexicans by more efficient Anglo miners. Arizona Copper Company, on the other hand, had both high- and low-grade ore, and could operate for a while on their high grade, but the workers' request, Lewis claimed, would shorten the life of that property by 50 percent. The editor of the *Copper Era,* the weekly newspaper of Clifton, argued that any settlement would have to depend on these facts.[11]

The average striker did not understand statistical explanations of what the companies could or could not afford any more than he understood the dispute over union recognition. He wanted higher pay, and he believed that through the strike he could obtain it. Almost daily, Miller, Moyer, and local leaders addressed the strikers, instilling enthusiasm, squelching rumors, and promulgating "official" policy. Mass meetings were held alternately at Clifton and Morenci. Workers in both communities got their exercise; the men marched to the "host" town and back again in parade formation. Picket duty and these gatherings constituted the only activity of the rank-and-file workers. The strike was now in its third week. The miners eyed their exhausted larders and hopefully looked for something to break the deadlock.

As soon as he learned of the managers' rejection of the miners' proposals, Sheriff Cash sent the governor a telegram informing him that the conference had been a hopeless failure and urging him to come to Clifton to help effect a settlement. Although he had been asked by both the companies and the men to visit the district, the governor replied that there was little that he could do "as the situation now stands." Nevertheless, he agreed to come and add his "voice and counsel to efforts toward peace" if another conference could be arranged. Without waiting for an answer to this message, Governor G. W. P. Hunt and his adjutant general left Phoenix by train for the strike area.[12]

George Wiley Paul Hunt was 55 years old when the strike began. He was born on November 1, 1859, at Huntsville, Missouri, a town founded by his grandfather. Although he prided himself on the social status of his ancestors — he claimed to be related to the first president through his father, George Washington Hunt, and to the second chief justice through his maternal grandfather, John Marshall Yates — Hunt grew up in poverty, his family having lost their money during the Civil War.[13]

When he was 18 he ran away from home and gradually made his way to Blackhawk, Colorado, where he worked for six months in a boardinghouse kitchen. In the spring of 1879, he set out for Santa Fe to work on the railroad, then journeyed to El Paso, Lordsburg, and finally to Shakespeare, New Mexico, where he found work in a mine. The mine soon played out, and he returned to boardinghouse work. On June 4, 1881,

Governor George W. P. Hunt
as he appeared in 1914.

Hunt and two companions left to try to find gold in Arizona. On Columbus Day he "packed a burro" into Globe, where he spent the next 2½ years as a waiter at the Old Pascoe Restaurant, became a member of the Waiters' Union, and took an active part in the affairs of that organization. In 1884 he got a job as a mucker at the Old Dominion Mine, and when it closed in 1886 the future governor went to San Francisco to work. In 1890 he returned to Globe and became a "delivery boy" for the Old Dominion Mercantile Company. Ten years later he was the president of the firm.[14]

While he was establishing himself as a successful businessman, Hunt became active in politics. He lost his first bid for elective office — county recorder — but two years later, in 1892, he was chosen a representative to the territorial legislature. He spent four years in the lower house and four years as Gila County representative in the Council before temporarily retiring from politics in 1900. Four years later the future governor was elected to a seat on the Council again, and served in the final three sessions of the territorial legislature. The Democrats, with control of the upper chamber in 1904 and 1908, chose Hunt as president. At the last session, Hunt and the other lawmakers shied away from progressive measures, lest they delay statehood.[15]

When President Taft signed the Enabling Act, union leaders, hoping to influence the constitutional convention in the interests of the working man, at first attempted to organize a labor party. As a third party, the labor group did not appear able to elect enough delegates to control the convention. Largely through intervention by Hunt, leaders of the two parties reached an agreement whereby the Laborites withdrew from politics and supported the Democratic Party, which in turn incorporated labor planks into its platform. The convention was called to order on October 19, 1910. With 41 Democrats to 11 Republicans, and Hunt as president, the meeting proceeded to adopt a liberal constitution. The following fall, G. W. P. Hunt was elected the first governor of the state.[16]

Hunt's motto, "Remember your friends, and forget your enemies," dictated the course of his political actions. Labor, an important cog in the so-called "Hunt Machine," benefited from its association with the "globular governor from Globe." Having worked the mines himself, Hunt knew the needs and wants of the worker; a successful businessman, he was sympathetic to the problems of the entrepreneur. He distrusted the "extremists" on either side, and attempted to steer a middle course, his sympathy all the times with the "underdog." A master politician, he captured the favor of the common people with bombastic problems and promises, by emphasizing his own humble origins, and by attacking the "interests" — that is, big corporations such as the railroads and copper companies. Hunt acquired a devoted following that never wavered in supporting both him and his deeds. He was almost constantly under attack from the press, yet his policies apparently pleased the "dodgasted persnicketiness" of the voters. He was elected seven times, and in later terms, his enemies referred to him as "George V, George VI, etc." [17]

The governor arrived at the train depot in Clifton Tuesday morning, September 28. He exchanged pleasantries with residents as he made his way to the Reardon Hotel, where he set up headquarters. The mine managers were the first delegation to call. Hunt told them that he was there to learn the facts and "call white white and black black." After he heard their side of the strike, the governor proposed an arbitration committee to be composed of the three managers, a representative of the workers from each company, and one disinterested person appointed by himself. Bennie, McLean, and Carmichael balked at this idea, and reiterated their insistence that any settlement must be preceded by the elimination of the federation from the district and a period in which they could observe the spirit of the men. When the managers asked Hunt to dine with them that evening, he declined, abruptly telling them that he came to end the strike, not to eat. [18]

After the union organizers exchanged their views with him, Hunt invited the workers to present their grievances personally. With a court reporter named Shortridge transcribing the testimony, Hunt spent the rest of the day listening to complaints — some real, some imaginary — from a steady stream of strikers anxious to unload their problems to a sympathetic ear. The hearings went on in Morenci on Wednesday. As the men continued to come, the chief executive, in his typical manner, said that he did not know when he would return to Phoenix, and that he might make Clifton the capital until the labor problem was cleared up. Later in the day Guy Miller announced a "monster mass meeting" to be held Thursday at five o'clock in Library Plaza in Clifton at which Governor Hunt would address the crowd. [19]

The plaza in Clifton started to hum with activity shortly after noon as workers from Morenci and Metcalf began pouring into town. Ushers from the strikers' committee took up positions to channel the crowd into an orderly assemblage. A Mexican orchestra provided entertainment, while chairs were hurriedly secured for an unexpectedly large number of female spectators. By four o'clock over a thousand persons were milling about, seeking the best spot to watch the proceedings. Surrounding telegraph poles afforded points of vantage as did a boxcar standing on a nearby siding. Many of the men wore homemade badges proclaiming, "Hurrah for Governor Hunt!"

At five o'clock, a large truck decorated with the national colors was driven slowly through the crowd to the center of the plaza. Over three thousand businessmen, clerks, wives, deputy sheriffs, and strikers had filled the square by the time organizer Miller climbed onto the truck and opened the meeting by calling for a voice vote and show of hands from those who wanted to hear Hunt. An auto was sent for the governor while Miller continued his remarks. When the featured speaker, escorted by ushers, began making his way through the crowd to the platform, Miller cut short his remarks and said to Hunt, "Governor, you are wanted over here, right over here." [20]

Hunt climbed onto the platform. A reporter and court stenographer Shortridge were seated on the front end of the truck to take down the speech. I. Gutiérrez de Lara, a federation organizer from Los Angeles, stood next to the governor ready to translate his remarks for the Mexicans in the audience. [21] As he started to speak, shouts of "Hurrah for Governor Hunt!" and three cheers were given. In his introductory comments, Hunt praised "your good sheriff Cash," and said how proud he was to have been elevated to his position by people who can "go ahead and demand what they think are their just rights in an orderly and law-abiding manner." Emphasizing his remarks by pounding his fists, he continued:

> For the past few days I have been interviewing the boys. . . . I find conditions existing here that require adjustment. I feel that the men who have charge of these great works will be amenable to reason, and I believe they will meet you on common ground. When I come back to this community and have to bring troops, the principal officers of the companies will be no different from the poorest Mexican they control. I hope all of you realize that I am going to have order if I have to call every troop we have in Arizona. I do not want to come to this district except to bear the olive branch of peace, but if war comes, you will have to abide by war. There never was a condition but that it couldn't be improved, and I feel that employers and employees can get together, and if they cannot get together peacefully, they will have to get together some other way, because I am going to see you people get together some way, if I have to put every one of you in the bull pen. [22]

The rotund governor's harangue obviously pleased the crowd; they frequently interrupted it with applause and shouts of ¡bien dicho! (well said!). He rambled on for a half hour, repetitiously praising the workers' efforts to improve their conditions, but warning them to maintain order. Finally he concluded that "the time has come when the men and women who toil in this district should have justice, and that is all the governor of this state asks for." [23]

When the applause for Hunt died down, Miller rose and pledged to go to the "bull pen" if necessary to get what the workers deserved. Then Wiley E. Jones, attorney-general of Arizona, reminisced about his coming into the district 23 years earlier and by hard work raising himself to his present position. Jones concluded that "God Almighty is on the side of the workingman in this controversy." G. A. Franz of the Becker-Franz Mercantile Company in Clifton told the strikers that he was with them as long as he had a dollar in his pocket. He advised the men "not to starve working, but if necessary starve fighting." By the time the final speaker, a Mexican, finished, darkness had fallen, and the crowd had largely dispersed. Governor Hunt traveled by auto to Lordsburg, where he caught the train for Phoenix.[24]

Hunt had given a fine, if somewhat partisan, performance in the district. The strikers were pleased with their governor and his speech. Others were not as enthusiastic. The editor of the *Arizona Daily Star* called his utterances a serious mistake. Pointing out that the speech was before people who understood little or no English and "translated very likely in a crude manner," the *Star* editor felt that Hunt's remarks were "doubtless" taken by the workers to mean that whatever happened, he would protect them. I. W. Spear, editor of the *Arizona Republican,* said the governor should realize that he represented neither side and that his job was to preserve law and order, not to encourage agitation. The editor of *Dunbar's Weekly,* on the other hand, found the lamentations of the "copper press" toward Hunt "amusing." Governor Hunt's encouragement to the strikers, he said, consisted of a pledge that everyone would be treated with equal fairness. Most disturbed by the governor's oration were the mine managers, who accused him of making "inflammatory speeches" that encouraged the strikers and made the Western Federation bolder.[25]

On Saturday morning, October 2, about two thousand persons gathered in front of the union hall. Headed by a drum corps, the strikers and some of their children marched down Chase Creek to the center of Clifton. Some of the men carried signs, "Mine Managers too Proud to Confer," "Carmichael, Bennie and McLean Want Us to Starve," and "We Will Fight Before We Will Starve." Several of the children had a banner: "Are You Going To Let Us Starve, Too?" The parade halted at the general offices of the Arizona Copper Company, where the managers were meeting with their attorneys. Some of the men were cheering for the union, while others were shouting, *¡Abajo Los Gerentes!* (Down With The Managers!), and shaking their fists.[26]

A mechanic named Dawson, who had refused to join the union, came down the road and was surrounded by the strikers. When the miners began to manhandle him, Sheriff Cash intervened and took him to the courthouse for safety. The parade formed again and marched down East Side Street to the home of Norman Carmichael, who had returned from the meeting in Clifton. The workers shouted for him and Bennie to come out and lead the procession. Unsuccessful, the strikers walked to Hill's Addition and then to Shannon Hill, two suburbs of Clifton, on the way back to the union hall where they disbanded shortly after one o'clock.[27]

When the 3:45 passenger train pulled into Clifton, engineer Tom Simpson and fireman Pike Penn were ordered to turn it around and prepare to return to Lordsburg immediately. They uncoupled the engine and backed it down to the bridge in Hill's Addition, where they were to pick up the mine managers and the companies' attorney, Ernest W. Lewis. The four men arrived by auto shortly after four o'clock and climbed on the back of the light engine. Enjoying the novelty of the situation, the managers waved good-bye to the pickets as they passed the smelters. At Guthrie they picked up a coach for the remainder of the trip.[28]

As soon as the strikers learned that the managers had gone, they attempted, through the sheriff's office, to bring them back. One of the men, Roman Armijo, appeared before Justice J. A. McWilliams and swore a complaint:

> Norman Carmichael, J. W. Bennie and Milton McLean are accused of the crime of riot committed as follows: the said Carmichael, Bennie, and McLean on or about the second day of October, 1915, in Greenlee county, Arizona, willfully, knowingly, unlawfully, maliciously, forcibly, and feloniously did then and there in a riotous, tumultuous, and violent manner, assemble themselves together and then and there in a riotous, tumultuous and violent manner, having then and there the present ability so to do, unlawfully attempt to and did then and there with force and violence, disturb the public peace.

Specifically, Armijo alleged that the managers had incited a riot by leaving. When McWilliams issued the warrant for their arrest, Sheriff Cash tried to have them stopped at Duncan, but the engine shot through the station. After he notified one of his deputies, Joe Larrieu, who was in Lordsburg, to have the managers arrested as fugitives from justice, Cash and a private citizen, M. A. Franz, took off by auto for the New Mexico town.[29]

When Cash and Franz arrived in Lordsburg about one o'clock in the morning, Larrieu was waiting with the managers. A justice of the peace named Marsailles immediately heard the fugitive-from-justice charge in the lobby of the Vendome Hotel. Attorney Lewis pleaded that the managers left because of a rumor that the strikers were planning to seize them and force a contract, and that Cash was going to put them in jail for their own protection. Marsailles dismissed the case for lack of evidence. He had no jurisdiction in the disturbing the peace charge, but he ruled that they were not fugitives from justice by leaving as they did. Cash tried to talk Bennie, McLean, and Carmichael into returning to Clifton; they refused and proceeded to El Paso, where they set up headquarters in the Paso del Norte Hotel. Later in the day the managers declared that they left because of the "incidents of the day and the temper of the strikers." They felt that their presence was a "constant and increasing source of irritation," which would have led to "bloodshed within 24 hours." [30]

With the managers gone from the district, the possibility of a quick settlement became remote. Until their departure, relief to the strikers had been carried out on a temporary basis and in the most expedient manner. Provisions that the miners had hoarded were supplemented with whatever local assistance was obtainable. Some money was collected from the union initiation fee, which was raised from two to five dollars on October 5. Miners were required to join to be eligible for relief, and many businessmen felt "compelled" to have their names on the list. [31]

At first families were given provisions at cost, while single men were fed at boardinghouses set up in the three towns. Since there was no strike fund and few men had any savings, they soon became dependent upon the voluntary assistance of sympathetic labor unions and individuals. Cattlemen in the district donated 40 "beeves" to be slaughtered at a rate of 2 daily, while a local bakery contributed 50 loaves of bread a day. On October 7, 50,000 pounds of flour and 40,000 pounds of beans arrived by rail in the district. Obtained on credit, the provisions were turned over to the executive committee for distribution to the needy. [32]

The number of persons dependent on relief increased rapidly as the strike wore on into the second month. On October 8 the relief committee reported feeding 224 families and 33 single men. By October 16 the figures had risen to 2,300 families and 130 bachelors. [33]

Central relief stations were set up in each of the three towns to distribute the supplies. Every day, long lines of strikers waited outside these depots where the basic essentials — flour, beans, coffee, salt, lard, and whatever meat that was available — were doled out to the men according to need. The station at Clifton distributed 2 tons of flour, 1 ton of beans, 400 pounds of coffee, 600 pounds of lard, and 300 pounds of salt on a typical day. At Morenci, the men were given 1 ton of flour, 1,000 pounds of beans, 600 pounds of lard, and 100 pounds of salt, while the Metcalf depot meted out 780 pounds of flour, 400 pounds of beans, 150 pounds of lard, and 50 pounds of salt per day. In Clifton the Union Restaurant, located opposite the relief depot, occasionally offered music for the bachelors' dining pleasure. The men enjoyed a meal to the strains of "Aloha" and "La Paloma," or watched the married men jauntily bearing sacks of flour and parcels of beans from the relief station to the "syncopated rhythm of a Charlie Chaplin walk."[34]

Other necessities were provided as required. Medical care was available at all times; shoes and clothing for the children were distributed whenever such contributions were received.[35]

The workers received assistance from many sources — including the companies. When the managers turned the mining properties over to the sheriff for protection, he hired strikers for guards. They were paid by the companies, and they turned over part of their earnings to the relief committee. The donation was apparently not voluntary; at least one man was run out of town when he refused to give 15 percent of his wages.[36]

Various unions rendered whatever assistance they could afford. At the convention of the Arizona State Federation of Labor in October, members were asked to help the miners. John T. Walker, president of the Illinois Federation of Labor, spoke in Clifton and pledged financial aid from his organization. Both the United Mine Workers and the American Federation of Labor solicited voluntary contributions from their affiliates, while the executive board of the Western Federation of Miners somewhat reluctantly voted $1,000 in November and encouraged local organizations to help as much as possible. The workers were told that the WF of M had levied an assessment of 50¢ per man and one day's wages per month on its members, but this turned out to be false.[37]

The bulk of aid came from the Globe-Miami mining district. The men there went all out to help their brothers in Clifton-Morenci. The workers subscribed to a fund of $2.00 a month per man; several merchants promised half a day's profit each month. The Ladies' Aid to the Strikers sponsored the usual benefit dances, dinners, clothing drives, and carnivals. A jeweler sold guesses for 10¢ apiece on the number of seeds in a pumpkin in his window; a ruby souvenir ring was the prize. Lester Doane, president of the Arizona State Federation of Labor, conducted a cake contest which netted the strike fund $1,500 and Mrs. Nellie Jones a 125-pound cake. Sandow, "the strongest man in the world," gave an exhibition in Miami. Lifting 700 pounds with one hand, and breaking chains by expanding his chest, he performed before a packed house and contributed 60 percent of the proceeds to the Greenlee County miners. By work and play, the people of Globe-Miami raised over $15,000, three-fourths of the total collected in the state.[38]

Voluntary assistance provided an adequate, but somewhat unstable, source of support. The union sought a more solid financial base. In mid-October the leaders of the strike began to agitate for a $150,000 county bond issue to feed the strikers. Since the mining companies paid 91 percent of the taxes, the organizers looked on this as a way of forcing these corporations to feed their former employees, and hence a means of hastening the end of the strike. Because of questions about the legality of such a proposal as well as the problem of who would buy the bonds, the plan was abandoned.[39]

The idea had come to the workers from Governor Hunt who announced early in the strike that if the people were starving, he would declare martial law and direct the Greenlee County Board of Supervisors to feed them. On October 1 the governor decided that he would feed them at the expense of the state if they needed food. By October 22 Hunt doubted that he could render financial assistance to the strikers because the legislature would have to make such appropriations "unless in the event of people starving to death."[40]

Delegates to the State Federation of Labor Convention urged the chief executive to take over the mines under the provisions of the Industrial Pursuits Act. E. W. Lewis quickly countered that Hunt would be personally liable for any damages or injury. In his typical fashion, the governor said the state had the right to operate the mines but that he did not intend to do it.[41] Lacking any legal means to help, Hunt lent his official voice to the call for aid on October 27 in a proclamation:

> Appealing to the people of Arizona for generous co-operation in relief of suffering families in the Clifton-Morenci mining district:
> This is the season of harvest, that especial time of the year when toll is taken of Nature's bounteous usufruct: when industries are measured in terms of their products; when Labor takes accounting of that which it produces; and when prosperity is carefully gauged in its relation to human endeavor. It is well if, at this period of the year when the day of Thanksgiving approaches, they who have plenty may freely celebrate their good fortune with the comforting assurance that the grim spectre of woeful want is not abroad anywhere in the land. For the observance of feastdays when the hungry go unfed, the homeless go unsheltered and the sorrowing go uncomforted must savour sharply of sacrilege, and ever be tinctured with sadness.
> In the Clifton-Morenci Mining District . . . there exists deplorably a condition whereby nearly five thousand workingmen are deprived of employment, and where consequently hundreds of families with their slender savings exhausted are entering upon the rigorous winter season without any dependable supply of the necessities of life. Words cannot express or pictures portray the extreme

suffering that even now is baring its cruel visage to the worthy people of this stricken district.

Pursuant, therefore, to the plain dictates of humanity, I . . . do herein proclaim the serious need of food, fuel, and clothing in the Clifton-Morenci district, and do earnestly appeal to the generous people of this state for such contributions of money and supplies as will alleviate suffering and afford means of simple sustenance for penniless families in this time of industrial trouble. All civic and benevolent organizations are especially urged to organize and conduct movements for the gathering and shipment of supplies to the Workmen's Relief Committee, care of the Sheriff of Greenlee County . . . to the end that, through ministrations unto those who are afflicted, the spirit of mercy and brotherly love may be exemplified in our citizenship.[42]

CHAPTER 3

Troops and Trouble

When the managers left, the district was virtually under the control of the miners. After seeing their passengers safely to Lordsburg, Pike Penn and Tom Simpson turned their light engine around and returned to Clifton. Since they operated with the approval of the Brotherhood of Locomotive Engineers, the two men saw nothing wrong in taking the mine managers from the district. The strikers felt otherwise. They thought that Bennie, McLean, and Carmichael were permanently abandoning their properties, and they were highly excited and embittered. As Penn and Simpson were walking home from the depot, they were "set on" in the dark by a mob with sticks and clubs. At about 11 o'clock on the evening of October 3, a gang of almost two hundred men with clubs and "missiles" showed up at Penn's house and advised him and Simpson to leave the district. Four deputy sheriffs guarded the home for the rest of the night. Early the next morning the two railroad employees left in an automobile for Duncan, "disregarding the speed limits." Later that day Morgan Merrill, an expressman, was "run out" of Clifton because he was a friend of Penn and Simpson.[1]

During the course of the strike, especially in the first month, many persons either felt it advisable to leave the district, or were advised to do so. Most of the foremen, shift bosses, and lesser officials of the companies found the first two weeks an excellent time to "take a vacation." Many persons who opposed the union or in some other way were inimical to the strikers voluntarily left for a healthier climate.[2]

The leaders attempted to get every worker to join the union or to leave. Most men complied with the request; those who did not were asked to come to union headquarters, where they were given some time to obey. Those who decided to go were given passes with such wording as *Favor de no molestar al Señor Grencacio Santa Cruz quien saldrá en 48 horas* (Please do not interfere with Mr. Grencacio Santa Cruz, who will leave in 48 hours). A similar pass, signed by Deputy Sheriff Alex Arnett, gave Nicholas Tardano 24 hours. Reluctant workers, intimidated with threats of violence, usually slipped out of town during the night, although a few waited until mobs visited them. None of these men suffered broken bones, but a few were considerably "roughed up." Most of the holdouts spent at least one night in jail under the protective custody of the sheriff before they could be transported safely out of the district.[3]

Sheriff Cash, with a force of about 50 deputies, feared that strict enforcement of the law would incense the 4,000 striking workers and lead to bloodshed. Lacking enough men to control the strikers should they become unruly, he adopted a policy designed to prevent violence by eliminating sources of irritation. Most of the deputies he appointed to protect the property of the companies were strikers, or at least sympathetic to them. Moreover, he kept a close watch on potential troublemakers, advised many of them to leave, and as a last resort, put them in the courthouse to protect them from harm.[4]

Pedro Michelena, a former Clifton resident, returned and began stirring up the Mexicans against the union. When a mob surrounded Michelena, Cash took him to jail and searched him. Finding letters from company representatives offering to pay his expenses, the sheriff told him to leave town. Joe Ritz, a leader of the sanitary gang of the Arizona Copper Company, was allowed to continue work after the strike began because of the nature of his job. One evening some 40 men called him from his home, accused him of deriding the union, and "worked him over." He escaped and hid under a nearby building. When he returned home, deputy sheriffs took him to jail for the night and put him on the train for Duncan the next morning.[5]

The first emigrants from the district had nowhere to go. Large numbers of them went to Duncan, 35 miles south of Clifton, where they rented whatever space was available. Some men sought employment in other mining areas; others went to El Paso looking for work. Most of those who left early in the strike were the lesser officials and skilled Anglo-Americans, men necessary for the resumption of operations once the walkout was over. The companies, therefore, set up a tent city shortly after the strike began for "relieving the embarrassment and distress" of the workers. Any former employee was welcome to come to the Duncan camp, where he was provided with free board, bed, and blanket. Company officials, who were given leaves of absence at half-pay, were invited, but they were expected to support themselves. Other residents of the district who felt compelled to leave received free ground for a tent.[6]

Frank McLean, brother of the general manager of the Detroit Copper Company, was put in charge of the tent city. "Mayor" McLean, as he liked to be called, had the difficult task of providing the necessities of life for the citizens of the "newest and fastest growing town in Arizona." Since most of the people had made hasty exits from the district, few came with anything but the clothes on their backs. McLean set up committees and work gangs to handle the various municipal functions, to provide relief, and to keep the men busy. For families, the building crew erected tents — each with pine floors and electric lights — along carefully laid out streets. Two bunk houses were constructed for single men. Families cooked in their tents; the bachelors ate at an old farmhouse which had been remodeled into a mess hall with a capacity of two hundred. Single men were given credit certificates for small necessities at Duncan stores; married men got additional vouchers for food. A "sanitary squad" was charged with disposing of garbage and keeping the streets of the town clean.[7]

In November "Mayor" McLean announced a contest to name the camp. He offered a ten-dollar prize and proclaimed himself the sole judge because, as he put it, "What's the use of being mayor of a town if you can't choose the name by which it is to be known to the historians of future generations?" One man suggested "Siesta" because all the men did was sleep. McLean apparently either did not like any of the appellations submitted or did not want to part with his ten dollars; he never made public the name he selected.[8]

As the number of residents increased, the amount of work required of each person decreased. When the men finished their daily tasks, they either went hunting or back to bed. The principal event of the day was the arrival of the morning train from Clifton. A few took advantage of the reading and writing tent, where a good supply of paper, pens, and stamped envelopes was available for the refugees to write back to their friends in the strike zone of the "joys of life in Duncan."[9]

The miners in Clifton and Morenci had other ideas about the Duncan colony. They believed that it was a camp for strikebreakers and that as soon as there were enough men the managers would bring them into the district and resume operations. The strikers contended that previous employment was not a prerequisite for enjoyment of the privileges of the encampment. Further, they insisted that men were being brought to Duncan to supplement the numbers there in order to gain sufficient strength to break the strike. Officials of the companies repeatedly denied any intention of using strikebreakers; they claimed that they refused admission to anyone not known to them.[10]

Charles W. Harris, adjutant general of the Arizona National Guard, sent an officer in the guise of a workman to the camp to investigate. The officer reported that he was admitted to the camp after being advised "to remember that he had worked for the companies." Once inside, he said that he talked to many persons who had come from other areas and that everyone expected to go to work as soon as there were enough men to enter the district. The spy that Harris sent was somewhat over-zealous. The adjutant general later modified his original charge, saying that the Duncan officials accepted the word of the men that they had previously worked for one of the companies.[11]

After the strike was settled, Governor Hunt admitted that Harris had been deceived. The miners imported from other areas, he said, were actually workers who had left the Clifton-Morenci area early in the strike to seek employment elsewhere, and finding none, went to Duncan for free food and lodging. Such an interpretation, however, did not allay the fears of the workers in the strike zone. They were sure that the companies would import "scabs" to end the walkout.[12]

In spite of what he may have discovered later, Governor Hunt was convinced throughout the walkout that the mine managers would attempt to use strikebreakers, and he was determined that they should not succeed. He did not believe that a large body of men would initiate and endure the hardships of a strike unless they were convinced that they had just grievances. Workers, he said, were entitled to fair consideration and adjustment of legitimate complaints, and they could not get this if "scabs" were permitted to take their jobs. He felt that a large strike in a mining or manufacturing community created unusual problems — problems that could not always be solved by "technical interpretations of law" or by individual claims by the strikebreaker to his constitutional right to work wherever he pleased. Hunt pointed out that, as industrial strife in Colorado in 1913 and 1914 had demonstrated, the importation of armed thugs and strikebreakers was an open invitation to bloodshed and wholesale destruction of property. In such cases Hunt thought every citizen's constitutional right of protection was more important than "theoretical contentions for individual liberties."[13]

Governor Hunt had been in daily contact with Sheriff Cash from the beginning of the strike. On October 2 Hunt announced that he would send troops if the walkout was not ended in one week and called on National Guard units in Phoenix, Tempe, Mesa, Tucson, and Yuma to be ready for action. He also ordered General Harris, on his way to Florida with the state rifle team, back to the capital. When he learned that Bennie, McLean, and Carmichael had left the district, the governor put an initial detachment of 48 men on alert and wired New Mexico Governor McDonald for permission to ship troops through Lordsburg.[14]

Both Hunt and the union leaders feared that if federal troops were stationed in the district, the managers, in spite of statements to the contrary, would attempt to use strikebreakers, and violence would result. Hunt was irritated because the managers fled from the state "in a manner so melodramatic, so true to the techniques of the movies as to suggest quite forcefully . . . that the theatrical effect was, after all, the object of the exodus." He contended that they wanted to give the public the impression that the strikers were lawless and desperate, thereby creating a situation favorable to the importation of armed guards and strikebreakers under military protection. As soon as Cash informed him that the managers would not return to Clifton, Hunt ordered the alerted contingent, under the command of Major H. H. Donkersley of Yuma, to proceed to the district.[15]

The guardsmen arrived in Clifton on Monday morning, October 4, to set up camp on the courthouse lawn. The Arizona Copper Company strikers welcomed them, and the next afternoon the miners from Morenci marched to the encampment to greet "Governor Hunt's troops." Donkersley said that the militia was sent to ensure that the companies would not "prevail on the president" to send in federal soldiers as a prelude to strikebreakers. The militiamen were available to be used at the discretion of Sheriff Cash for "any unforeseen emergency that might arise." Since there were no riots, and the troops were not even being used for guard duty, the major saw no need for additional soldiers. The next day he and Cash went to the state capital to confer with the governor. Despite Donkersley's earlier statement, on October 7 100 more men were ordered to the district, including 47 Apache Indians of Company F of Phoenix. Two days later 40 men from Flagstaff left for Clifton. Hunt explained that the additional troops were sent to convince the managers that it was safe to return.[16]

When the second contingent arrived at their campsite, they found themselves in an abandoned cemetery one half mile south of Clifton on a rocky hillside overlooking the main road to the district. The coffins had been removed several years earlier, leaving a pockmarked pasture of partially filled graves. The men cleared about three acres, leveled the ground, and set up their tents in neat rows, not unlike the interment plots they replaced. Several of the graves were redug to serve as latrines. Down the hill, a tent with a slanting board floor and shower baths was erected. Since the men in Clifton used the showers in the county jail, all the guardsmen were in a "constant state of next-to-godliness." [17]

Local YMCA leaders opened a tent and supplied writing tablets, newspapers, chocolates, and other refreshments to help the men pass their leisure time. Captain Holyworth, a former teacher, conducted night classes for three militiamen who were high school students from Tucson. Eight university men had to keep up with their studies on their own. The troops spent each day practicing military tactics, performing menial tasks, and polishing their Springfields, which were loaded and ready for use at a moment's notice. [18]

The presence of troops in the district was a cause for curiosity rather than concern on the part of the strikers. The miners had continued their activities under the watchful eyes of Sheriff Cash, the union leaders, and now the military. Fortunately, saloons had been closed since January 1, when Arizona adopted prohibition; the taverns on Chase Creek in Clifton had been among the wildest in the state. The elimination of liquor had removed a potential problem that could have caused serious incidents had it been allowed to inflame the passions of four thousand workers. Cash eased the men along, interfering only when trouble appeared imminent. [19]

The leaders were anxious to avoid any incidents, especially ones that would discredit the union or cause the militia to be used. They were particularly worried that the Mexicans or "less intelligent whites" would disregard their commands. The organizers carefully avoided making inflammatory remarks in their speeches. In one harangue, however, Tribolet, one of the first union men to come to the camp, became violent against the companies and capital in general; he obeyed a "polite request" to leave the district. On October 6 the local union officials issued instructions that in the future, any member who committed a misdemeanor or in any way brought "reflections of wrong-doing" on the union would be brought before them to "answer in full" for such actions. "Intimidation, fighting with non-union men, destruction of property, and misuse of legal rights" were classified as such activities. [20]

The issuance of these instructions was prompted by a series of acts which threatened to disrupt the amicable relations between Cash and the union. On October 3 José Padilla, postmaster of Steeple Rock, New Mexico, went to Clifton to see a doctor. Mistaken for a strikebreaker, he was attacked by a mob of 300 men and severely beaten. The sheriff took him to the hospital, where he remained for four days with two broken ribs. That night, 50 men entered the Arizona Copper Company electric plant, overpowered the engineer, and switched off the power. Under the cover of darkness, another group broke the windows in the company drug store and the general office building. Company officials said the drug store incident was an obvious attempt to intimidate store employees to join the union. They threatened to close the facilities if the union persisted. The next day the companies shut down their offices, boarded the windows, and gave the clerks leaves of absence at half-pay.[21]

The afternoon of October 4, a "monster parade" was held in Clifton with two bands and about three thousand marchers. In the evening the water main between Morenci and Newtown was dynamited by unknown persons. The strikers disavowed any connection with the incident and called it "part of a plot to starve them." They repaired the line. Early on October 5, someone opened the gates of the reservoir at the Arizona Company concentrator, emptying the huge water storehouse. Later that day several hundred Mexicans stormed through Morenci demanding union cards of everyone.[22]

On October 11 the businessmen of Morenci requested that some of the militia be sent there. Deputy Sheriff Larrieu, acting for Cash who was in El Paso trying to arrange a bargaining conference, feared that such a move might arouse the anger of the Mexicans. He advised against it, saying he felt troops were not needed at that time.[23]

Although kept in a constant state of readiness, the troops had nothing to do but the dull daily duties of encampment. To pass some of their off-duty hours, the Apaches of Company F competed with Clifton High School in football on October 16. The Indians, most of them only two years out of high school, won 27-6. The victory was credited to the size of the guardsmen, but "the speed of the young ones caught up toward the end of the game." The following Wednesday morning, the National Guard scheduled a field meet against the high school.[24]

While the troops were running foot races and playing baseball, four hundred strikers were demonstrating outside the Reardon Hotel, where James Casey, general counsel for the companies, and M. "Biddy" Doyle, "chief of police" at the Duncan camp, were staying. The two men had come to town to secure affidavits about conditions in the district; the miners heard that they were passing out train tickets to Duncan and sounding out persons on returning to work. Casey and Doyle left on the evening train. In the afternoon the strikers held another parade in Clifton. Over two thousand workers marched to the bakery of Frank

Salarni, an opponent of the Western Federation. After the band played the funeral dirge, the crowd moved to the courthouse to serenade Sheriff Cash and then went on to the militia campsite south of town. There the musicians entertained the troops with patriotic airs, and the demonstration ended with a salute to the flag.[25]

The camaraderie between the troops and the townspeople did little to combat a growing dissatisfaction on the part of the guardsmen. On October 18 notices were posted that, as provided in the *Military Code of Arizona,* after 30 days of continuous service the rates of pay would be the same as for like grades in the regular army. Instead of a $1.50 per day, for example, privates would earn $17.00 per month. The next day State Auditor J. C. Callaghan announced that he was not sure that there even were funds to pay the men. Because of legal complications, he said, they might have to be issued certificates like those given the guardsmen who went to the annual encampment and the bandsmen who went to the San Diego and San Francisco expositions.[26]

In June a special session of the legislature had passed the general appropriations bill with a provision that if the governor vetoed any items in the bill, such veto would not revive the statutory appropriation for those items. It also banned the auditor from drawing on any fund unless authorized by the legislature. The lawmakers were attempting to repeal statutory appropriations and to substitute lower ones. Hunt vetoed numerous items as well as the repealing clauses in the bill. Since there was a question as to whether the governor could annul such limitations, or if the legislature even had the right to pass such provisions, Callaghan was advised to pay no money out under any sections in question until the Arizona Supreme Court passed on the bill. Because of this legal squabble, the guardsmen did not meet for three weeks after summer camp, and had not yet received any money for the certificates issued during the annual encampment. On October 21 the troops on duty in Clifton learned that they would continue to get these warrants until the supreme court, not scheduled to meet until December 9, ruled on the tangle between the governor and the legislature.[27]

Governor Hunt had been under criticism from the editors of almost every newspaper in the state for the problems arising out of the controversy over the appropriations bill as well as for his opposition to capital punishment and his desire for penal reform. The use of troops in the strike zone added to his difficulties with the press. C. H. Akers of the *Arizona Gazette* said Hunt and WF of M leaders were trying to get control of the state, and called the governor's actions "the worst sort of politics." The editor of the *Tucson Citizen* attacked Hunt for his poor economy in sending only part of the Guard to the area in order to keep the cost down. He said that it would have been better to send no troops at all than a "wholly inadequate force." I. W. Spear of the *Arizona Republican,* on the other hand, condemned the continued presence of soldiers in Clifton as a waste of money since there were no disorders and nothing was being done to prevent the deportation of men.[28]

From outside the state, the editor of the *El Paso Herald* called Hunt's actions "Arizona's Shame." He felt that Arizona was still passing through a period of "radicalism and bold experimentation in governmental practices" to which the rest of the country could either assume an attitude of "amused tolerance" or take a genuine interest in the "efforts of the new state to find itself." An editorial in Tucson's *Arizona Daily Star* quoted the *Pueblo Tribune* which advised Hunt to study recent Colorado history. Warning the chief executive that the Western Federation was a criminal organization, the writer noted that Hunt was "playing with fire" by encouraging the union instead of insisting that all citizens recognize the law.[29]

On October 22 a movement for the recall of Governor Hunt — said to have been the first such action against the chief executive of a state — was announced in Mesa. There had been talk of removing Hunt earlier in the year. During the special session of the legislature that passed the appropriations bill, conservative Democrats considered it as a means of getting rid of the "extravagant Hunt" lest they face the prospects of dwindling political fortunes in the next elections. In July the discussion was revived over the governor's stand on capital punishment. By mid-October Democrats began to worry that the little popularity Hunt gained among the 12 percent mining population for his activities in the strike was more that offset by losses among other citizens for the same actions. All this talk was translated into a concrete proposal with the Mesa movement.[30]

The leaders of the recall movement were C. H. Akers of the *Arizona Gazette,* O. S. Stapley, Democratic state senator from Mesa, and R. F. Johnson, a rancher from the Mesa area. They had organized the campaign in Phoenix, but moved the drive because they wanted it to spring up outside the capital and not in a mining camp. They thereby hoped to disassociate it as much as possible from the mining interests and broaden the base of support by making it appear a "grass roots" movement.[31]

On October 26 the Mesa Commercial Club passed a resolution to work for the recall. Akers said that petitions would be wired all over the state by the Associated Press. About 65 members walked out following the presentation of the proposed motion. When the club met on October 28, a heated debate developed over the recall. Hunt supporters claimed that the petition was outside the organization's bylaws which forbade action on political or partisan questions; advocates of the move countered that the recall was for the betterment of Mesa. By a 14-vote margin the club rescinded its action, but this did not end the affair.[32]

A recall petition had been drawn up for presentation to Arizona Secretary of State Sidney Osborne. It claimed that Hunt was incompetent to perform his duties or conserve the peace and dignity of Arizona, charged him with wanton and reckless extravagance, and accused him of setting himself above the law. The document contended that he had "deliberately attempted to foment and encourage class hatreds and divisions," and that, by a "program of unconcealed and deliberate catering to the most radical elements," the governor had "created a condition approaching anarchy in certain sections of the state."[33]

Hunt fought back with bitter denunciations of the three leaders of the recall movement, and with an accusation of his own. He described Stapley as a "humble lackey of certain interests in the Senate," and called Johnson a "disappointed office-seeker seeking revenge." Akers, a Republican, had supported the governor in 1914. A year later he called the chief executive dishonest, and he was characterized by Hunt as a "despicable turncoat and timeserver, the abject tool of a few corporate interests." In questioning his honesty, Hunt said Akers had lied "just as his wretched excuse for a newspaper" had done for a long time. The governor said the recall movement was a "political sortie" to discredit his efforts to have a federal investigation of the Clifton situation. Calling the charges "glittering generalities," he warned the men at the head of the affair that he was going to make public some "important documents" that he thought would make "interesting reading."[34]

Hunt had obtained several telegrams which proved that some newspapers in the state were being paid to print advertising as news, a violation of postal regulations. On October 15 the managers at El Paso had made public 35 affidavits from men who had left the district either by orders of the union or because they feared violence. The same day Ned Creighton, owner of the Arizona News Service, had sent telegrams to newspaper editors throughout the state offering to pay them to publish a full page, including cuts of strike scenes and the affidavits, on the "truth about the Clifton-Morenci strike conditions." The copy was not to be "labeled advertisement or marked in any way to indicate same as paid matter, as written copy will clearly state part taken by the Western Federation of Miners in trouble and object of publishing is to make clear why companies in the district refused to deal with the Western Federation." The editor of the *Santa Cruz Patagonian* had been offered $10.50 to run the story. Hunt threatened to expose the sham and have those guilty prosecuted. The newspapers that favored turning Hunt out of office had all carried the story, and the recall matter died.[35]

The stubborn Hunt was not intimidated by the recall movement. Two days after the Mesa movement began, perhaps partially to spite his critics, the governor ordered an additional one hundred troops to Clifton. At the same time, he released the students and a few businessmen from active duty. While the troops were on their way, a committee composed of W. T. Witt, chairman of the Greenlee County Board of Supervisors, B. F. Billingsley, a prominent merchant, and B. R. Lanneau, cashier of the Bank of Duncan, addressed a strikers' rally and assured the men that there were no strikebreakers at the Duncan camp; they would not be tolerated. Sheriff Cash and Major Donkersley confirmed these statements for the men. The meeting was held amid increased concern that strikebreakers would be brought into the district. On October 20 a rumor that a hundred refugees were coming to Clifton sent a thousand miners to the Arizona Copper Company smelter one mile south of town to prevent their entry. No such force appeared, and it was hoped that this rally and more guardsmen would allay such fears.[36]

With the arrival of the latest contingent, approximately one-third of the Arizona National Guard was in the district. The new arrivals were temporarily split between the two existing camps until October 29 at four o'clock in the morning when one hundred men, under the command of Major E. P. Grinstead, marched the seven miles to Morenci and set up camp without incident. The strike was now costing the state $1,000 a day, and with the exception of a spectacular fire that did $150,000 damage to the Arizona Copper Company concentrator, activities were almost routine — constant rumors, a daily parade, and an occasional deportation. Even the fire caused no great storm. Company officials refused to make accusations, and the strikers blamed the blaze on defective wiring. They pointed out that it was a striker who sounded the alarm and that several miners were injured battling the flames.[37]

By November 8 the governor was convinced that local authorities could handle the situation. Lacking funds to pay the soldiers or justification for keeping them, Hunt released 250 guardsmen from active duty. Four days later he withdrew the Indians of Company F, leaving only a token force of 60 men in Clifton.[38]

When the troops left Clifton, there was widespread talk among the dissatisfied men that they would not come out again if called for strike duty because they had been compelled to serve without pay. This meant that if serious trouble developed in the district, federal forces would probably have to be sent, because the few remaining guardsmen would be

inadequate to handle any major difficulty. Union leaders, especially concerned that federal intervention be prevented, doubled their efforts to keep
the men in line and to dispel any stories about disorders.[39]

In late October the strikers had attempted to keep people from
leaving the area. After the Guard left, the number of emigrants increased,
for the miners were anxious to prevent adverse publicity by forcing them
to stay. The mine managers believed that the flow of from 20 to 50
"refugees" daily into Duncan meant that the "backbone of the strike
would soon be broken." They wanted to do nothing, therefore, that
would disrupt the bloodless nature of the strike. The militia, it would
appear, were accomplishing more by their absence than they had by
their presence.[40]

CHAPTER 4

Negotiations

While the two sides continued to eye one another with suspicion, go-betweens were busy trying to get the managers and miners together. On Tuesday, October 5, Homan C. Myles, the British consul at El Paso, requested that J. W. Bennie, an English subject, be given safe conduct to Phoenix to confer with Governor Hunt. Bennie was concerned that he might be arrested on the inciting-to-riot charge if he returned to Arizona. The governor replied that as long as Bennie violated no law he would be welcome, and he granted him an interview on Thursday morning. That same day Hunt sent a letter to the managers asking them to meet with the strikers. He told the three men that he could see no justification for their refusal to hold a conference, especially since the workers had agreed to renounce the Western Federation. He called their other two conditions — that the influence of the WF of M be dissipated and favorable conditions for the resumption of operations be established — a "state of mind over which there was no control." Bennie came as far as Lordsburg, where he met with company representatives, but he refused to cross the state line.[1]

It was when Hunt learned that Bennie was not coming that he had ordered the second contingent of troops into the strike zone on October 7. Sheriff Cash, Major Donkersley, and Adjutant General Harris, who were in Phoenix conferring on the situation, accompanied the militiamen as far as Lordsburg. Donkersley took the soldiers the rest of the way; Cash and Harris went to El Paso with another letter from the governor to the managers. In this missive, Hunt told the three men that his purpose in writing was to advise them of new conditions in the district. He said that he had "positive assurances" that the seven Western Federation organizers in Clifton "will have voluntarily withdrawn themselves . . . by the time this communication shall have been delivered into your hands." Furthermore, with the National Guard in the district, the managers could return home safely and settle the dispute.[2]

The sheriff and the adjutant general arrived at El Paso Friday morning, October 8. Harris told a reporter he was there on a pleasure trip and winked. E. E. Ellinwood, a company attorney, said the two men were passing through on the way to Clifton. Cash and Harris went into a long conference with McLean. That afternoon they discussed arrangements for negotiations with all three managers, and were given a letter for the governor.[3]

In their response to Hunt, the companies accused him of making "inflammatory speeches" and "openly encouraging affiliation with the Western Federation." The note went on to reiterate the earlier position of the copper concerns — that they would resume operations only when the "atmosphere is entirely clarified of the dominating influence of the Western Federation under whatever name, title, or disguise it may take." Bearing this reply, Cash and Harris returned to Clifton the next morning.[4]

Cash had wired his under-sheriff, Henry Hill, from El Paso that the managers would meet with their former employees, and by the time he and Harris arrived in the strike zone, union leaders already had begun making arrangements to send a delegation to Texas. Hill had notified the presidents of the three locals, Juan Guerra of Clifton, Abran Rico of Morenci, and Carlos Carbajal of Metcalf, to choose a committee to represent them. Many of the men were opposed to leaving the district for a conference because they felt that this would put them at a disadvantage. Others argued that if they refused, they would lose sympathy and support in the state.[5]

At a mass meeting on Saturday, Cash told the workers the conditions for the confab as transmitted to the governor. At the same time he announced the names of the seven men selected to go to El Paso. At first the sheriff named only six miners: Frank T. Tarbel, Frank Hocker, and Dick Walsh, representing the workers of the Arizona Copper Company;

Amos C. Bean and Norberto Gonzales from the Shannon Company; and Abran Rico for the Detroit Company employees. The Mexicans from Clifton, however, insisted that Guerra be included, and he was made a delegate-at-large.[6]

After the meeting Cash wired the managers the names of the men who were being sent. Norman Carmichael sent a telegram back stating that the persons selected were unsatisfactory. The sheriff did not reveal the contents of this message to the strikers. Instead he called the managers, explained that the situation in the district was grave, and persuaded them to let the delegates come to El Paso. Accompanied by Harris and Cash, the group left Sunday morning for Texas.[7]

While the delegation was on its way to El Paso, Bennie, McLean, and Carmichael changed their minds. When the seven men got to the Paso del Norte Hotel, the managers refused to meet with them, claiming that two of the men were officials of the Western Federation and that one was a discharged employee. They handed Harris a memorandum which stated that they would meet a committee of five men selected by them from a list of names previously submitted to discuss "such grievances as the committee may submit." The delegation was to have no officials or prominent agitators of the federation in it, and two members were to be Mexicans. The rejected representatives returned to Clifton that same afternoon.[8]

The men in the strike zone were disappointed by the abortive mission, but they agreed to make new concessions, mainly because Governor Hunt urged them to do so. On October 13, 15 men were selected, and the list of names was sent to El Paso. The next day the managers announced that they had chosen J. S. Hughes, Theodore Hollingsworth, Henry Daly, Rufino García, and Adolfo Palacio to meet with them. The companies consented to pay their expenses. This new delegation was instructed by the union leaders to concede all points except a pay raise, a minimum wage, a guarantee against discharge for strike activity, and the right to affiliate with the Western Federation. The miners were not demanding recognition of the WF of M, but merely the right to affiliate. Any agreement by the group was to be subject to ratification by the workers. The five men, accompanied by Cash and Harris, left by train for Texas early Friday morning and arrived in El Paso that evening.[9]

Saturday the two sides held a brief organizational meeting. Harris asked to be admitted to the session as a representative of Governor Hunt, but he was barred by the managers; attorneys for the companies also withdrew. Henry Daly, chairman of the delegation, declared that the men had agreed to waive formal recognition of the Western Federation, and he presented a proposed wage scale, which the managers said they would study.[10]

Monday morning the men discussed the reinstatement of workers discharged between September 1 and 11. The managers said they would practice no discrimination against union men, but reserved the right to fire persons "perniciously" active in agitation among the miners. A dispute arose over several discharged employees. The managers called them agitators; the strikers said they were organizers. At the conclusion of the confab, the company spokesmen asked the employees to change their demands on several points and to meet again the following day.[11]

Tuesday the miners offered a plan to return to work under a new wage scale and to arbitrate the rest of the issues. They suggested binding arbitration, with two workers, two managers, and one representative from the Department of Labor deciding the cases. The managers rejected this idea, but the discussions continued for the rest of the week. When the executive committee in the district learned that the managers would answer the employees' proposals on Saturday, they announced that they would issue no more instructions to the delegates in Texas. They decided to let the El Paso committeemen use their own discretion in offering a "rock bottom" proposition to the managers' reply.[12]

The week-long conference came to an end on Saturday afternoon when the managers handed the strikers' committee a written statement. In it the three company leaders claimed that the Western Federation was influencing the miners' delegation in all its work. The managers once again stated their position — the federation had to be eliminated in both body and spirit from the district, and the men had to return to work before they would discuss any question or grievance.[13]

The strikers called the conference a "farcical affair." They claimed that the companies had prolonged the meetings by "managerial pretense and deception" in an attempt to starve them into submission. When they learned that the office help of the Shannon Company was taken off the payroll the day before the conference ended, they took this as a sign that the managers had not expected the mission to El Paso to be a success. The workers stated that the federation organizers had left the district but were continuing to aid the union in such functions as relief solicitation because the local organization would be "helpless" without outside assistance.[14]

The local union organization began to suffer internal dissension almost as soon as the federation advisers left the district. Many of the Anglo workers had never been very enthusiastic about the strike. On

October 23 the executive committee issued orders that every picket party must include at least two or three Anglos. That morning the Mexicans at Metcalf announced that they were going to try to get the Anglos to participate in their next parade. (A reporter for the *Arizona Republican* speculated that the effort was "not likely to be a success.") [15]

In the afternoon, Juan Guerra, president of the Clifton local, and Ricardo Rodríguez, secretary, resigned to avoid being recalled. Guerra was accused of "treachery" for saying that he absolutely controlled the Mexican strikers and could send them back to work at any time and under any conditions suitable to himself. Rodríguez suffered guilt by association. The two men were put in jail, released once, but returned to jail the next day after strikers beat them up. The miners did not want them to leave the district because of the information they knew, and neither of the men dared go to Duncan because of the many enemies they had there. They remained in jail for the duration of the strike. [16]

A week later Frank Tarbel and George McKenzie, leaders in the Morenci local, were arrested for disturbing the peace. They had entered a meeting of ten men appointed to audit the union books and had tried to confiscate the ledgers. These defections caused a temporary loss of confidence by the strikers in their leadership. [17]

The Guerra incident occurred at an unfortunate time — the day the El Paso conference ended. On October 25 Sheriff Cash offered a new plan to end the impasse between the strikers and the managers. The proposal called for the men to return to work immediately and have all the issues settled by an arbitration board. In Clifton, only 26 men voted against the proposition; at Metcalf and Morenci, when union leaders tried to explain it, the Mexicans booed and jeered. They accused their leaders of being Guerra backers and rejected the deal. [18]

Although many miners had decided before all this trouble that any hope for a settlement lay in a federal investigation of their grievances, distrust of their leaders seemed to have solidified that feeling. On October 7 Governor Hunt had requested that Secretary of Labor William B. Wilson order an investigation of the strike. Wilson subsequently had appointed Joseph S. Myers, a federal conciliator, to go to Arizona and look over the situation. When Myers arrived in Phoenix, the first delegation was on its way to El Paso. He announced that the Labor Department would not intrude in the strike zone or enter into the negotiations unless "all other means of breaking a deadlock have failed." [19]

Workmen in the district, meanwhile, had begun agitating for the secretary of labor to order an investigation, while the executive committee began collecting evidence to present, should such an inquiry be held. When the El Paso conference failed, Myers had tendered the managers the services of the Labor Department in helping adjust the difficulties. On October 26, after all attempts at settlement had apparently been exhausted, Wilson wired Hunt that he had asked Myers and Hywell Davies, another conciliator, to make a "thorough examination of conditions existing in the mining industry of Arizona." The conciliators spent the next month collecting data in Phoenix, various mining camps, and El Paso, before going to Clifton.[20]

While Myers and Davies quietly went about their work, the businessmen of the district, suffering from the depression resulting from the strike, became active in seeking an end to the deadlock. In early October, the merchants had sent John Christy, state representative from Greenlee County, to attempt a settlement. He was well received by the managers in El Paso, but when he appeared before the Arizona Federation of Labor Convention at Tucson, hoping to persuade that body to intervene and put pressure on the Western Federation to end the walkout, he nearly started a riot by calling the strikers "barbarians" and Hunt a "wooden Indian." By the time the inept Christy arrived in Phoenix, he had become useless as a mediator. The governor granted him a brief interview that ended with Hunt abruptly telling him that if he, Hunt, were not governor, he would "take him out in the grounds and beat the stuffing out of him." Like the strikers, the businessmen now put their hopes in a federal investigation or another conference, while their trade continued to drop.[21]

By the first of November the financial slump had affected almost every business in the community. The loss of the mining companies' monthly payroll of $450,000 had drained the district of its monetary blood. Grocery and drug store sales were only a trickle of their former volume; clothing store owners reported almost no customers. Mexican widows who had done washing or housework when the mines were operating were forced to get relief from the strike committee. Most of the movie houses managed to stay open, but the "for hire" auto service, which catered to Mexican workers who liked to rent a big car and take it for drives through the countryside, closed down. The library and pool halls were about the only businesses that were prospering.[22]

On November 19 about one hundred Greenlee County businessmen met at the Clifton Town Hall to discuss the strike situation and to see if some steps could be taken by them to help end the stalemate. They appointed a mediation committee to sound out both sides and report in one week. Meanwhile, Myers and Davies arrived in the district and began taking testimony from the strikers behind closed doors at the courthouse. When the merchants gathered the following Thursday, the mediation commission reported that they had received encouraging replies from both the managers and the miners. Since some of the businessmen felt that any action on their part might impede the work of the Labor Department, the group decided to "maintain their organization and resume negotiations as soon as possible after the report of the U.S. representatives." [23]

Myers and Davies had no sooner arrived in the district than new trouble began to plague the area. Sheriff Cash had taken over the power plants in September when the strike began. The companies had continued to collect the bills and to pay the men. As non-union or nonsympathetic workers left the district, Cash had hired strikers and expanded the size of the crews. In November the companies refused to pay these men, and they walked off the job, plunging the towns into darkness for one night.[24]

The sheriff protested to the Arizona Corporation Commission, which regulated public utilities. The commission sided with the mine managers and demanded that Cash explain why he was running the power plants without their knowledge. Company officials agreed to pay the men, however, and they gave Cash a voucher bearing the endorsement "paid under protest." Fearing that he might be held liable, the sheriff refused to pass the wages on to the men, but they assented to continue working.[25]

A more serious event occurred on November 25, four days after Myers and Davies reached Clifton: a fatality ended the bloodless character of the ten-week walkout. A worker, Casimiro Martínez, returned from Duncan for some of his personal effects. He was confronted at the train depot by pickets who accused him of being a strikebreaker and ordered him to go to union headquarters. He refused and made his way to a house on Burro Alley, followed by a crowd. When Lusano Ramírez tried to take him from the home, Martínez shot him.[26]

Five days later Andreas Telles Gondera, a clerk at the Phelps Dodge Mercantile Store, was accosted on his way to work by 20 men. They pinned a sign, *esquirol* (scab), on him and paraded him from Morenci to Clifton. After they beat him up, he was marched out of town and ordered not to return. L. J. Owens, manager of the store, called the sheriff's office to protest and was told that there were no deputies available to come to Gondera's aid. Later in the day the Phelps Dodge employees wired Governor Hunt that they were not being given adequate protection. Hunt replied that Cash and the National Guard were doing their utmost for the citizens and that any deficiencies in security were due to the failure of the county board of supervisors to provide enough deputies.[27]

Prompted by the Gondera deportation, one hundred businessmen met at the schoolhouse in south Clifton on Friday night, December 10. They formed the Clifton Citizen's League, "a species of a vigilance committee," for mutual protection against riots and disorders and to safeguard lives and property. The group drew up a resolution to be presented to the town council asking that all members be made deputy marshals. The council recognized the league on Monday, and made all its members deputies subject to the call of the town marshal. About 200 residents were sworn in late in December, but because there were no disorders, they were never called to duty. On December 17, however, the county board of supervisors approved a request by the organization for eight more regular deputies for Sheriff Cash.[28]

At the December 10 meeting, the businessmen also reactivated their mediation board to try to get the managers and miners together. The following week the board sponsored a series of discussions in Morenci between union leaders and company spokesmen. The first two meetings were described as friendly, but the Western Federation proved to be the "stumbling block" to any agreement. A third conference, scheduled for December 17, was called off when the company representatives failed to appear.[29]

As the end of the year approached, the outlook for a peaceful end to the walkout appeared grim. For almost two months the two sides had not even met, and there seemed to be no prospect for an amicable settlement in the near future. Events that month made it appear to the workers that the strike might be broken. Twice in December about 250 miners had "held up" trains coming to Clifton and searched them for strikebreakers. Since both trains carried mail, such acts were federal offenses. After the threat of an investigation by postal officials and possible federal intervention, the strikers stopped this activity.[30]

A more serious threat of outside intervention occurred on December 18 when attorneys for the Detroit Copper Company filed a petition in the federal court at Tucson asking for an injunction restraining the unions from interference with assessment work on the company's unpatented claims. The copper firm had 140 plots which under federal law were held on condition that $100 worth of work be done annually on each of them. The company chose to survey them each year at a cost of $100 per claim in order to retain possession. Sheriff Cash had assured Frank McLean that the work could be done, but when the superintendent showed up to make the arrangements, Cash told him he feared that violence would result if the work was attempted. Judge W. H. Sawtelle ordered 21 union leaders to appear at a hearing on December 24 to show cause why the assessment work should not be done.[31]

The leaders of the strike saw the assessment work as a pretense by the managers to have federal troops brought into the district. At the hearing attorneys for the union argued that the company could not appeal to a court until actually prevented from doing the work. Moreover, they contended that the plaintiffs could not lose title to the claims if prevented by force from making the assessments. Company lawyers countered that their client had a right to have the work done irrespective of the strike, and that court action did not have to wait for an overt act.[32]

Sheriff Cash testified that there were reliable contractors in the community willing to do the work, but he refused to name any. If the companies were allowed to import assessors, Cash admitted that he would be unable to prevent violence. On cross-examination, the sheriff revealed that Captain Hall of the National Guard was drilling some of the strikers as a "pastime," but pointed out that they did not have guns. Judge Sawtelle, nevertheless, sided with the company and granted a temporary injunction. The strike issue, he said, did not really enter into the merits of the case. U.S. Marshal Joseph Dillon and 50 deputies were ordered to go to Morenci the next day to see that the court order was carried out.[33]

While Judge Sawtelle was hearing final arguments in Tucson, the people in the district were holding a giant Christmas party. Because of their financial situation the strikers decided to have a municipal tree and community gathering. A special fund was set up to see that all the children were remembered. A huge tree from the Blue Mountains was set up in the plaza at Clifton, and a Mexican orchestra and local talent provided the entertainment.[34]

The Christmas spirit provided a temporary truce between the district and the Duncan camp. The refugees extended an invitation to the public to come to their "town" for the holiday. On Christmas Eve a grand ball was given at the Duncan theater. The next morning contests and games were held for the young; that afternoon a ball game pitted a Mexican nine against a team of Anglos. A big dinner was served from two to six o'clock, and candy and presents were distributed to the children. Several hundred strikers and their families took advantage of the free train ride to Duncan; a few decided to stay and enjoy the hospitality permanently.[35]

The day after Christmas, Dillon and his deputies arrived in Morenci and covered the district with notices of the injunction in both English and Spanish. On Christmas Day the Detroit officials had offered the strikers an opportunity as individuals to work the claims at five dollars a day. Only 14 men applied, reportedly because of pressure from the Western Federation not to accept. The following Monday 236 Duncanites were brought to Morenci to start the assessing, and Tuesday 250 more arrived without incident. Dillon searched the men for weapons and returned all that he found when the workers went back to the refugee camp.[36]

Union officials were extremely careful to avoid any trouble lest they be cited for contempt or cause the entry of federal troops to enforce the court order. The deputies kept a close watch on the assessors. One man tried to make an anti-union speech, and Dillon quickly put him in jail. The work lasted two weeks. On January 7, 250 men returned to Duncan; the rest left the next morning. Officials at the Duncan camp reported that an additional one hundred men were counted when the assessors came back. On the night before the federal officers left, the strikers held an appreciation demonstration for them. A Mexican band serenaded the men and several union leaders gave speeches of "thanks and praise to Dillon and the deputies."[37]

While the assessment work was progressing in Morenci, events elsewhere were paving the way for a settlement. The strike was proving costly for both sides. The price of copper had risen from 17.375¢ per pound the day the strike was called to 22.50¢ on December 31. While other mining areas were enjoying this prosperity, the Clifton-Morenci camp stood idle. Over 1½ million dollars in wages alone had been lost by the miners.[38]

On December 22 the federal investigators had concluded their hearings and had gone to El Paso to submit a proposition to the managers. From there, Myers and Davies went to Washington to confer with Secretary Wilson and then to New York to talk to the directors of Phelps Dodge. In the final issue of the *Copper Era* for 1915, the Arizona Copper Company Store Department, somewhat ironically perhaps, ran a half-page advertisement wishing all its customers "A Year of Continued Prosperity and Success."[39]

On New Year's Day the managers submitted a proposition through Henry Hill and Reese R. Webster of the citizen's mediation committee. They offered to adjust the sliding scale to include wage increases when copper sold for 20¢ a pound and over and to resume operations at once if the workers surrendered their charters with the Western Federation. The next day the strikers agreed to give up affiliation with the federation, but they rejected the proposal because the wage increase was too small. It would have amounted to about 5 percent, while copper prices had advanced 15 percent. The Anglos accepted it almost to a man, but the Mexicans turned it down almost unanimously.[40]

Doctor A. V. Dye, representing the managers, addressed the workers at Morenci on Sunday, January 23, and asked them to end their alignment with the Western Federation. On Tuesday he spoke to the miners in Clifton. No conclusive action was taken at either meeting, but the executive committee told Dye to ask the companies to hold the offer open for one week so they could eliminate the WF of M in a bona fide manner and select a delegation to go to Texas. Hill and Webster returned to El Paso where the managers agreed on January 8 to advance the sliding scale to include 24¢ copper if the other conditions were met.[41]

The two citizen mediators returned to the district on January 9, and the next day they explained the proposition to mass meetings of the workers. In exchange for the new wage scale, the men were to give up the Western Federation and return to work immediately. No strikers were to be fired except those guilty of violence, and the number that could be discharged for this reason was to be limited to ten for all three companies. Finally, after resumption of normal operations, the managers would meet their employees.[42]

On January 11, four months after the walkout began, the miners formally renounced the Western Federation. About one thousand persons attended the ceremony in Library Plaza. The executive committee handed the charters and seals of the three locals to a delegation of citizens. They in turn gave them to Sheriff Cash to be sent to WF of M headquarters in Denver. The strikers then threw away their union cards and swore allegiance to the Arizona State Federation of Labor. Finally John L. Donnelly, vice-president of the state federation, addressed the crowd.[43]

He told the men that they should be proud of their fight to organize, and that he was happy to represent them in the negotiations with their employers. The strikers, he said, had complied with the demands of the companies, and the next move was up to the managers.[44]

Bennie, McLean, and Carmichael remained silent in El Paso while spokesmen and mediators maintained a dialogue between the two sides. Myers and Davies, back from the East, conferred with Governor Hunt in Phoenix and then went to Texas, where they reviewed the proposed settlement with the managers and Hill and Webster. Meanwhile, on January 17 the miners voted to return to work for 15 days, provided that a conference be held during that period. In addition, they stipulated that no employee who refused to join the union or went to Duncan be employed during that interval. When the managers refused to accept this condition, the miners agreed to a gradual importation of refugees at the discretion of Cash, Hill, and Webster. On January 21 the federal mediators went over the plan with the managers and then left for Clifton to recommend its adoption by the strikers.[45]

On Sunday, January 23, a mass meeting was held at the Princess Theatre in Clifton to discuss the managers' offer. John Donnelly told the men that he would not advise them one way or the other, but that if it were up to him, he would not accept the settlement. Hywell Davies reminded the miners of the impartial nature of the Department of Labor and then reviewed the financial condition of the strikers. He told the workers that they could expect little or no more help from other union organizations. Finally he explained the terms of the "Hill-Webster proposition," as the January 8 proposal of the managers was called, and recommended that the men compromise and take it as the best deal they could get. A move to return to work was defeated by 28 votes because many strikers wanted more time to study the terms and to permit the Morenci and Metcalf miners to pass on it first. The next morning the men at Metcalf unanimously approved resumption of operations; that afternoon the Morenci miners sanctioned the proposal. The Clifton workers voted again that evening, and the strike was ended.[46]

CHAPTER 5

Aftermath of the Strike

On Wednesday morning, January 26, the whistles blew in the Clifton-Morenci district for the first time in 4½ months. The shrill sound summoned only a small number of workers, but it was cause for general rejoicing. About two hundred men held an impromptu celebration in Morenci when the call for work was heard. The managers had returned earlier to supervise the start-up; the mules and horses were expected back from Safford on Thursday. The workers who made a preliminary inspection of the mines found most levels dry and ready for ore to be shoveled into the chutes; only a few areas had flooded. The first of some 1,300 refugees from Duncan began arriving on the afternoon train. They feared trouble when they returned to the district and had written to Governor Hunt for protection. He had replied that it was up to the Greenlee County authorities to provide such security. It was not needed; they entered with only minor friction. Merchants kept the wires hot all day ordering supplies as the area once again took on the aspect of activity and industry.[1]

By the end of the week, two thousand men were back on the payroll, and it was "confidently predicted" that within 30 days all the workers would be reinstated. The last of the National Guard forces left Clifton on Monday, and by Friday the number of employed went above three thousand. On Wednesday there was a brief strike at Metcalf over the hiring of Duncan men, but the matter was quickly adjusted. Myers and Davies, who were ordered to stay in the state for six months to assist in the final settlement and to keep in touch with the situation, met with the managers twice during the week to discuss plans for the conference with the workers. John Donnelly also remained to aid the miners in their negotiations and to help effect an orderly resumption of operations.[2]

The transition from idleness to industry was accomplished with little difficulty; few exceptions marred the conversion. On February 11 the employees of the Detroit Copper Company walked out when a foreman hired a new man before all the old employees were working. Donnelly advised the men to return to work pending an investigation and warned the minor officials to live up to the spirit of the agreement, as the managers were doing. Bennie shut down the Shannon Company concentrator and leacher for "repairs" when he heard of a threatened walkout, and this interruption lasted three days. The editor of the *Copper Era* admonished the workers for boycotting various institutions and individuals. He reminded the men that their statement at the conclusion of the strike called for the spirit of the brotherhood of man in the community.[3]

In spite of these problems, the district was almost back to normal by February 17 when the managers and the union began to work on the final agreement. At the first conference 17 representatives of the miners, the 3 managers, the 2 federal investigators, and A. T. Thomson, assistant manager of Phelps Dodge, met in the office of the Arizona Copper Company. For the next five weeks similar discussions were held. On February 25 the men announced agreement on a new wage scale effective March 1. By its terms employees received raises of 5 to 15 percent, depending on the job. A minimum wage of $2.00 per shift was established, and the sliding scale, based on the price of copper, was formally adopted. At the same time discrimination in salary between Mexicans and Anglos was ended.[4]

The new scale meant a tremendous boost in wages. A laborer had earned $1.92 per day when the strike began. For the first period after the walkout, he made $2.12. In February this rose to $2.52 per shift, based on the January average of 24¢ copper. With a wage hike under the final settlement, and the rise in copper prices to 26¢, his earnings were $3.08 in March. A miner had made $2.89 per day in September 1915; for his first pay period in 1916, he received $3.08. In February this was up to $3.53, and his pay after the agreement was $4.01 per shift.[5]

After another month of negotiations, the final pact was worked out. In addition to readjusting the wage scale upward, it banned the Western Federation from the district, although it affirmed the right of affiliation with any other union. It also set up procedures for airing grievances. A committee was created to investigate individual complaints and to try to settle them with shift bosses or foremen before appealing to the managers. Anyone agitating a strike or quitting work before a final decision was handed down was to be subject to discharge. For complaints affecting the whole community, a joint grievance committee of 12 was organized. Finally, the agreement provided discharge for any company official who accepted or demanded gratuities from any worker as the price of employment, and it acknowledged the men's right to buy wherever they chose. On March 29 the three managers signed the contract for their companies; Theodore Hollingsworth and C. S. Edmondson endorsed it for the union.[6]

The workers were satisfied with their new contract; they were earning the highest wages ever paid in the district. Considering that copper prices had soared to an all-time peak however, the pay hike was not really a tremendous victory. The salary increases, while substantial, were much less than the minimum wage of $2.50 per day for surface laborers and $3.00 for underground work that the men had requested, and practically nil compared to inflated copper prices. The average monthly price of the metal had risen 56 percent from August 1915 to February 1916. The pay increases represented a 39 percent advance for miners and a 60 percent advance for laborers. Donnelly said that winning the right to organize was the "big thing," but even this was questionable, since the union conformed almost completely to the terms laid down by the managers.[7]

By their persistence, Bennie, McLean, and Carmichael had succeeded in preventing the establishment of the Western Federation in the district. On the other hand, their properties had been closed down for five months at a time when copper was selling at the highest prices in eight years. The strike was especially detrimental to the profits of the companies in 1915 because copper prices were low during the first part of the year. The rapid rise in the price of the metal as the year ended benefited the companies in wage negotiations by allowing the managers to grant a small increase in pay which appeared to the workers as a substantial salary hike because of the sliding scale. Fortunately for the managers, the price of copper remained high throughout 1916. By the end of the year, copper prices had risen to 33.50¢ a pound. Laborers were then earning $3.91 per shift, more than double what they made when the strike began.[8]

Wages consequently ceased to be a major cause of labor difficulties for the rest of the year. Other problems, however, came to the fore to plague peaceful relations between the managers and the miners. In the 18 months following the settlement, workers staged 17 strikes in various departments of the three companies. Superintendents and other officials complained that they were constantly occupied with investigations and grievance meetings. Any attempt to fire a man was a cause for trouble. The miners also found fault with company hiring practices. They maintained that the company surgeons placed "too much diagnostic importance on the cerebrations of strong union tendencies" in pre-employment physicals. On one occasion they protested when the Detroit Copper Company refused to give the union land in Morenci for a union hall.[9]

The biggest problem, however, was efficiency. Norman Carmichael complained that production fell from 2.60 tons a man per shift in 1915 to 2.22 tons in 1916. At the same time the average wage per shift had gone from $2.34 to $3.72. The union organization which the managers had permitted was proving stronger than they had anticipated.[10]

In February the executive committee of the Arizona State Federation of Labor granted a charter to the miners of the district. They set up the Clifton District Labor Council and began a drive to organize all of the crafts in the area. One month later they had a membership of over four thousand workers and had $9,000 in the bank. The miners voluntarily assessed themselves a day's wages per month for half a year in order to pay back some $25,000 worth of bills which they had incurred during the strike. The men were taking their union commitments seriously. In six months they had passed from no organization at all into a formidable group conscious of the power of collective action.[11]

The persons responsible for unionism in the district left before they could reap the benefits of their efforts. When the Western Federation of Miners withdrew, the strike committee expressed their appreciation to Charles H. Moyer, saying, "You have done all in your power to save us." After the walkout was settled, they had second thoughts. In July the annual convention of the WF of M was held at Great Falls, Montana. For several months prior to the meeting, a running battle had been waged over the actions of federation officials in Clifton. As part of a "new blood" movement in the organization, George Powell, president of the Miami Miners' Union, was trying to unseat Moyer as head of the federation. He and his followers attempted to capitalize on Moyer's actions in Clifton. They accused him of repudiating the miners and obtained the aid of the strike committee to discredit his activities. Nevertheless, Moyer beat Powell by a three-to-two margin in the election.[12]

Of more interest and concern to the people of Clifton and Morenci were the state and county elections of 1916. On March 30 Governor Hunt announced that he would be a candidate for a third term. He claimed that human liberties were the issue in the campaign because "popular government in Arizona is in danger of being dethroned and supplanted by a hierarchy of special interests." Labor organizations immediately came to his support. Hunt Clubs, composed mostly of wage-earners, were formed throughout the state. With the Clifton-Morenci strike as the latest reminder, these groups were repaying Hunt for the cooperation he had given the labor movement in his first two terms. The Arizona State Federation of Labor closed its annual convention with a unanimous vote endorsing the governor's reelection.[13]

Organized labor's support of Hunt was a major issue in the campaign. Many persons still remembered the $35,000 he had spent sending troops to Clifton to prevent the importation of strikebreakers who never appeared. The editor of the *Arizona Daily Star* saw a Hunt victory as a threat to the future prosperity of the state. With its large, undeveloped resources, Arizona needed capital and "Hunt's Socialism," the editor lamented, "is a danger that makes even northern Mexico a more attractive place to invest." Spear of the *Republican* said the Hunt campaign was based on the idea of aligning class against class. He supported Hunt's opponent, State Tax Commissioner Thomas E. Campbell, a native of Prescott and the only Republican candidate elected in 1914. Hunt countered the press criticism by a personal tour of the state to tell the people "things the copper-subsidized press won't tell you." When he spoke in Clifton, he was greeted with several banners, including one calling him the "Juárez and Hidalgo of the Mexicans in Arizona."[14]

The people went to the polls on November 6. When the official results were tabulated, they showed that Campbell had won by a slim 30 votes out of 58,000 ballots cast. At the urging of friends, Hunt demanded a recount. He later claimed that he "was loathe to have this done, but there had been so much skulduggery in the campaign that I finally consented."[15]

The problem centered around ticket-splitting. In Maricopa County a large number of persons had marked their ballots straight Democratic and then placed an "X" before Campbell's name. These ballots had been counted for Campbell. In Gila and Greenlee counties, many people had voted straight Democratic except for sheriff. In these cases the ballots had been thrown out. Sheriff Cash was defeated by A. H. Slaughter 908 to 889. He protested that he should receive all the votes marked straight Democratic in spite of the marking for his opponent.[16]

Ironically, if a uniform standard was used, Hunt could not lose. If all the contested sheriff and gubernatorial ballots were thrown out, he would win; if they were all included, he would still win. According to Arizona law, the Democrats should have received the votes where straight Democrat was marked, even if people marked names in the Republican column. While legal action was being initiated, Campbell demanded and received a certificate of election from the secretary of state.[17]

On January 1, 1917, Thomas Campbell went to the Capitol Building to be inaugurated. When he got to the door, deputy sheriffs from Maricopa County barred the entrance and told the governor-elect that the Capitol was closed because it was a holiday. Campbell appealed to the superior court and became *de facto* governor on January 29 after that body declared him the winner. His salary was held in abeyance, however, pending the outcome of a suit which Hunt took to the state supreme court. The justices heard arguments regarding this suit in October and handed down a ruling on December 22 which declared Hunt the winner. Although he "felt sorry" for Campbell, Hunt, nevertheless, on December 25, 1917, assumed the Republican's office and accepted his year's salary.[18]

In a sense the inauguration in Phoenix on Christmas morning, 1917, was the last of the results of the Clifton-Morenci strike. Even though it took place almost two years after the settlement, the strike had almost as great an influence on Hunt's political fortunes as he had had on the strike.

A "hunt" of a different nature also had a lingering effect. E. W. Kewaugh of the forester's office at Albuquerque reported that forages by strikers had greatly depleted the game supply in the nearby national forests. Men from the district alone had bagged 475 deer. The farmers of Greenlee County, on the other hand, were happy to report that the miners had killed all the rabbits in the area.[19]

The strike had been one of the most remarkable that had occurred in any mining region in the country. It was notable for its order and for the absence of bloodshed or property destruction. According to Myers and Davies, it was "conducted on a different plane to any Western strike of similar magnitude and duration."[20]

Many persons and groups either took credit for the peaceful nature of events in the district or were praised for their actions. Temperance societies said it all was an example of the benefits of prohibition. They claimed that the Mexican children were better fed and clothed during the strike than they had been when their fathers were working and Arizona had the open saloon. Socialists said the strike demonstrated the validity of their doctrines by showing the control three men had over the lives of five thousand miners and their families. The miners believed that Governor Hunt and Sheriff Cash deserved credit for the pacific nature of the strike because of their refusal to allow the importation of scabs. The managers contended that this was undeserved praise since the companies had no intention of introducing strikebreakers.[21]

No one faction or person deserved credit for either the peaceful nature of the strike or the final settlement of it. Both sides hurled charges at each other, but both sides showed restraint when it came to action. The strike began peacefully, and the miners and the managers wanted to keep it that way. By the time negotiations reached an impasse, Governor Hunt had moved to prevent the managers from breaking the strike. At the same time, the Department of Labor had entered the situation and given the miners hope that they would get a fair hearing of their grievances. Meanwhile the rise in copper prices and the loss of wages made a settlement desirable for both sides. The youngest state had given a commendable representation of itself in its first major labor difficulty.

Notes to the Text

CHAPTER 1

[1] *Bisbee Daily Review*, October 24, 1915; *Copper Era* (Clifton), September 17, 1915. The strikers refused to allow the mules of any of the companies to be fed or hoisted to the surface until persuaded by the sheriff to permit the animals to be taken out of the mines. *(Arizona Daily Star* [Tucson], September 29, 1915.)

[2] *Arizona Daily Star*, October 24, 1915; *Daily Silver Belt* (Miami), September 24, 1915; *Copper Era*, September 17, 1915; *Tucson Citizen*, October 5, 1915. Cash interpreted this arrangement to mean that he should run the power plants. *(Copper Era,* November 26, 1915.)

[3] Clifton was named for Henry Clifton, a gold prospector who came into the area in 1864. (James H. McClintock, *Arizona, the Youngest State* [Chicago: S. J. Clarke Publishing Co., 1916], 2, 421.)

[4] James Monroe Patton, "The History of Clifton" (master's thesis, University of Arizona, 1945), 5; "Greenlee's Mines and Farms," *Arizona, the State Magazine,* November 1914, 27. Morenci was named after Morenci, Michigan, believed to have been either the birthplace or home of Eben B. Ward, a wealthy steamship owner, who founded the Detroit Company in 1872. (Roberta Watt, "The History of Morenci" [master's thesis, University of Arizona, 1956], 23–24.)

[5] W. H. Weed, "The Arizona Copper Company," *The Mines Handbook and Copper Handbook, 1916* (New York: n.p., 1916), 168.

[6] Robert Glass Cleland, *History of Phelps Dodge, 1834–1950* (New York: Alfred A. Knopf, 1952), 81–84, 112–13.

[7] *Mining Journal*, May 30, 1929, 8.

[8] "Greenlee's Mines and Farms," *Arizona, the State Magazine,* November 1914, 14.

9 "Some Observations on Arizona Strikes," *Engineering and Mining Journal,* October 13, 1917, 642. (Journal hereafter cited as *E&MJ.*)

10 *Mining and Scientific Press,* November 11, 1915; *New York Call,* November 17, 1915 (taken from Governor George W. P. Hunt's Scrapbooks, vol. 19, 126, Special Collections, University of Arizona Library, Tucson. Scrapbooks hereafter cited as Hunt). Article by R. L. Byrd, *El Paso Herald,* October 12, 1915, and article by Walter Doudra, *El Paso Herald,* n.d., 1915 (both articles in Hunt, vol. 18, 43). It is interesting to note that during the walkout most of the independent merchants sided with the miners. A few backed the strikers to the point of bankruptcy. (*Arizona Republican* [Phoenix], November 1, 1915.)

11 Byrd, *El Paso Herald; Arizona Republican,* November 1, 1915.

12 Union officials claimed that the rates paid for water were higher than this, but a check of payroll records shows these to be the correct figures. After the strike the companies discontinued deducting water fees from the workers' pay. (Arizona Copper Company Payroll Records, 1914–16, Special Collections, University of Arizona Library.)

13 *Copper Era,* December 3, 1915.

14 *Arizona Republican,* October 9, 1915; Byrd, *El Paso Herald,* October 12, 1915. The rates given here are from the hospital directors. They are at variance with a statement by Walter Douglas, managing director of Phelps Dodge, who claimed single men paid $1.00 a month and married men $1.50. (*Arizona Daily Star,* September 29, 1915.) The directors said they received about $4,500 per month in dues alone, but that the hospital lost from $3,000 to $4,000 in 1914. R. L. Byrd said the fees withheld were $2,500 to $3,000 a month to pay the expenses of a hospital with less than 15 patients a month, 2 physicians, 2 nurses, and a cook. He was obviously referring to the Detroit Company Hospital in Morenci. The objections in the strike were mainly against the Clifton Hospital. (*El Paso Herald,* October 12, 1915.)

15 *Arizona Republican,* October 9, 1915.

16 *Arizona Daily Star,* September 29, October 12, 1915; B. F. Fly, article in unknown newspaper (Hunt, vol. 18, 6).

17 *Arizona Republican,* November 1, 1915; *El Paso Herald,* October 12, 1915.

18 "A Strike Without Disorder," *New Republic,* January 22, 1916, 304; *Copper Era,* February 5, 1915; *E&MJ,* February 5, 1915; Arizona Copper Company Payroll Records, 1914–16.

19 *Copper Era,* March 3, 1914; *Des Moines News* (Iowa), January 10, 1916 (Hunt, vol. 19, 47). As to the "safety" of mining investments, government figures released in 1916 showed that 36 percent of legitimate mining ventures failed against 54 percent in commercial lines, while the following returns on capital were earned: railroads, 3 percent; national banks, 6¼ percent; insurance, 11 percent; lumbering, 14 percent; manufacturing, 14 percent; mining, 182 percent. (*Arizona Daily Star,* January 29, 1916.)

20 *Copper Era,* August 7, 1914. United States production of copper in 1914 totaled 1,158,581,876 pounds, of which Arizona contributed 387,978,852 pounds. (*E&MJ,* January 9, 1915, 51.)

21 Arizona Copper Company Payroll Records, 1914; *Arizona Daily Star,* October 12, 1915; *E&MJ,* February 20, 1915, 387.

22 *E&MJ,* March 20, 1915, 546.

23 Arizona Copper Company Payroll Records, 1915. The managers claimed that the "15¢ and over" rate corresponded to when copper sold at 17¢, but the statement failed to list the rates. (*Copper Era,* February 5, 1915.) This lack of published schedules lends some credence to the complaint of some miners that often the same job paid different rates. (*Arizona Republican,* October 4, 1915.) A more plausible explanation for the disparities seems to be the amount of the "kick back" to the foreman.

24 *Copper Era,* January 14, 1916; Arizona Copper Company Payroll Records, 1915; *E&MJ,* July 19, 1915.

25 Article by Byrd, *El Paso Herald*, October 12, 1915 (Hunt, vol. 18, 43); *Copper Era*, September 24, 1915; *Arizona Republican*, October 24, 1915; Vernon H. Jensen, *Heritage of Conflict* (Ithaca, New York: Cornell University Press, 1950); Paul F. Brissenden, *The I. W. W.* (New York: Columbia University Press, 1920). The Western Federation of Miners changed its name in June 1916 to the International Union of Mine Mill and Smelter Workers.

26 In December 1915, the United States Supreme Court declared the 80 percent law unconstitutional.

27 Jensen, *Heritage of Conflict*, 141, 340; *Copper Era*, August 20, 1915. *Arizona Record* (Globe), September 4, 1915; *Tucson Citizen*, October 15, 1915.

28 *Copper Era*, May 8, November 6, 1914, August 20, 1915; *Arizona Record*, September 5, 1915.

29 *Copper Era*, August 27, 1915.

30 Arizona Copper Company Payroll Records, 1915; *Arizona Republican*, September 17, 1915; "Arizona Copper Miners Strike," *E&MJ*, October 9, 1915, 606; *Copper Era*, October 1, 1915. The rehiring of all employees discharged from September 1 to September 11 was a major consideration in the eventual settlement of the strike.

31 *Copper Era*, September 10, 1915.

32 *Douglas Daily International*, September 18, 1915.

CHAPTER 2

1 Jensen, *Heritage of Conflict*, 289–365.

2 *Copper Era*, September 17, 1915.

3 *New Republic*, January 22, 1916, 305; *Douglas Daily International*, November 29, 1915.

4 *Arizona Daily Star*, September 22, 1915.

5 *Arizona Republican*, September 23, 1915. The delegates from the Arizona Copper Company were C. S. Edmondson, H. J. McCarty, Juan Guerra, Duke Walsh, F. B. Hocker, H. O. Duval, Louis Soto, Ben Kirk, Henry Labeaux, Florence Navárez, and Frank Tarbel. The Detroit Copper employees chose J. D. O'Brien, Album Ruiz, C. O. Smith, Emilo Truja, C. J. Waddell, Francisco Lozano, A. Y. Smith, Antonio Hernández, with P. M. Vargas as interpreter. Shannon Company workers selected Aurelio Valdez, Norberto Gonzales, A. C. Bean, A. T. Aitken, José Uranza, Panteleon Vásquez, and Guillermo Vega, with G. S. Robertson, delegate-at-large. (*Copper Era*, September 24, 1915.)

6 *Tucson Citizen*, September 23, 1915.

7 Charles H. Moyer had become president of the Western Federation in 1903, and he was to serve as its head until forced to resign in 1926. In those 23 years he would see the federation gradually decline as, one by one, locals deserted the organization. Much of the blame for the disintegration was laid at Moyer's door. He was accused by the membership of lacking drive and of relying too much on the advice of a handful of confidants. In his desire to expand the size of the union, he often took on more than he could successfully handle at one time. (Jensen, *Heritage of Conflict*, 71, 462–64.)

8 *Arizona Republican*, September 26, 1915; *Daily Silver Belt*, September 25, 1915.

9 "Clifton-Morenci Strike, 1915–16," a collection of letters, statements, and articles on the strike. Special Collections, University of Arizona Library, Tucson.

10 *Arizona Republican*, September 27, 1915; *E&MJ*, January 23, 1915, 201.

11 *Douglas Daily International*, October 6, 1915; *Copper Era*, October 15, 1915.

12 *Arizona Republican*, September 28, 1915.

13 Sidney Kartus, "The Autobiography of George Wiley Paul Hunt," *Arizona Historical Review*, January 1933, 253.

[14] Peter Clark MacFarlane, "The Galahad of Arizona: Governor Hunt," *Collier's,* April 15, 1916, 21; *Denver Labor,* November 27, 1915 (Hunt, vol. 19, 107); Frank C. Lockwood, *Arizona Characters* (Los Angeles: Times Mirror Press, 1928), 194.

[15] Alan V. Johnson, "Governor G. W. P. Hunt and Organized Labor" (master's thesis, University of Arizona, 1964), 20.

[16] Tru Anthony McGinnis, "The Influence of Organized Labor on the Making of the Arizona Constitution" (master's thesis, University of Arizona, 1930), 30, 33.

[17] Lockwood, 194, 201, 208; MacFarlane, 21, 23; Samuel L. Pattee, "Governor Hunt — A Personal Appreciation," *Arizona Historical Review,* April 1935, 47; Waldo E. Waltz, "Arizona: A State of New-Old Frontiers," in *Rocky Mountain Politics,* Thomas C. Donnelly, ed. (Albuquerque: University of New Mexico Press, 1940), 285.

[18] Hunt Diary, September 28, 1915 (The Hunt Diaries, Arizona State University Library, Tempe); *Copper Era,* October 1, 1915; *Arizona Republican,* October 2, 1915.

[19] *Copper Era,* October 1, 1915. Hunt claimed that he interviewed "fully six hundred men" during his comparatively brief stay in the district. *(Arizona Republican,* October 2, 1915.)

[20] *Copper Era,* October 1, 1915.

[21] de Lara, a Socialist, was said to have been private secretary to Pancho Villa at one time. (*Copper Era,* October 1, 1915.) Another report claims that he quit the Madero army after the battle of Casas Grandes because "he could not stand to see his brothers killed." (Article in unknown newspaper [Hunt, vol. 18, 45].)

[22] "Clifton-Morenci Strike, 1915–1916." The "bull pen" reference was to stockade enclosures which were first used in a strike in the Coeur d'Alene mines in 1892. Union men and sympathizers were rounded up and held in these, pending trial.

[23] *Ibid.; Copper Era,* October 1, 1915.

[24] *Arizona Republican,* October 1, 1915; *Copper Era,* October 1, 1915. God and Wiley Jones may have been on the side of the workers then, but two weeks later before the U.S. Supreme Court, only God was. Jones went to Washington shortly after this speech to argue the validity of the so-called 80 percent law. He cited the Clifton strike as an example of the need for such a law, as the walkout demonstrated the need for closer exercise of the police powers of the state. (*Arizona Daily Star,* October 16, 1915.)

[25] *Arizona Daily Star,* October 8, 1915; *Arizona Republican,* October 5, 1915; *Dunbar's Weekly,* n.d. (Hunt, vol. 18, 50); *Tucson Citizen,* October 9, 1915.

[26] *Copper Era,* October 8, 1915; *Arizona Republican,* October 3, 1915; *Daily Silver Belt,* October 2, 1915; *Arizona Gazette* (Phoenix), October 3, 1915 (Hunt, vol. 18, 57).

[27] *Arizona Gazette,* October 3, 1915 (Hunt, vol. 18, 57).

[28] *Ibid.*

[29] *Copper Era,* October 8, 1915; *Arizona Republican,* October 4, 1915.

[30] *Ibid.*

[31] *Arizona Republican,* October 13, 1915.

[32] *Ibid.,* October 6, 1915.

[33] *Ibid.,* October 9, 17, 1915.

[34] *Ibid.,* October 23, 1915; *Daily Silver Belt,* October 19, 1915.

[35] *Ibid.*

[36] *New Republic,* March 18, 1916, 185; *Arizona Republican,* January 1, 1916.

[37] *Arizona Republican,* November 5, 1915, January 25, 1916; *Official Proceedings, Twenty-second Annual Convention,* Western Federation of Miners, Great Falls, Montana, 1916, 15.

[38] *Daily Silver Belt,* October 22, November 6, 1915; January 26, 27, 1916.

[39] *Douglas Daily International,* October 15, 1915.

40 *Tucson Citizen*, September 17, 1915; *Arizona Daily Star*, October 2, 1915; *Arizona Republican*, October 27, 1915.

41 *Arizona Republican*, October 7, 8, 1915. Actually Hunt could not invoke the Industrial Pursuits Act because the legislature had made no provisions for putting it into effect. (*Tucson Citizen*, October 8, 1915.)

42 *Copper Era*, October 29, 1915.

CHAPTER 3

1 *New Republic*, March 18, 1916, 186; *Copper Era*, October 8, 1915; *Arizona Republican*, October 5, 1915. Penn later was run out of Duncan for trying to organize one hundred cowboys to "clean out" Clifton. (*Arizona Republican*, October 8, 1915.)

2 *Tucson Citizen*, October 5, 1915.

3 *Ibid.*, October 12, 1915; *Arizona Daily Star*, October 19, 1915.

4 *Arizona Daily Star*, October 12, 1915.

5 *Ibid.*, October 23, 1915; *Daily Silver Belt*, September 27, 1915.

6 *Arizona Republican*, October 29, 1915; *Copper Era*, December 3, 1915; *Tucson Citizen*, October 12, 1915.

7 *Arizona Daily Star*, November 2, 3, 1915.

8 *Ibid.*, November 2, 1915.

9 *Arizona Republican*, October 29, 1915.

10 *Ibid.*

11 *Arizona Republican*, November 26, 1915; *Copper Era*, December 3, 1915. Charles Wilfred Harris was born in Garrett, Indiana, in 1879. He entered the army as a private in 1898, and joined the Arizona National Guard in 1903, also as a private. He was appointed adjutant general on July 3, 1912. (General Order 16, 5 August 1949, Death Notices of Adjutant Generals, National Guard File, Arizona Pioneers' Historical Society [Society hereafter cited as APHS].)

12 *New Republic*, March 18, 1916, 186.

13 *The Survey*, May 6, 1916, 146; *New Republic*, January 22, 1916, 305.

14 *Arizona Republican*, October 3, 1915.

15 *Ibid.; Denver Labor*, November 27, 1915 (Hunt, vol. 18, 107); *New Republic*, January 22, 1916, 304. Both federal and state troops had been used in the past to help break strikes. Because of Hunt's attitude toward labor and his statements during the first three weeks of the walkout, the managers could not have expected him to use state troops to protect strikebreakers.

16 *Arizona Republican*, October 5, 6, 8, 1915; Governor Hunt's letter to managers, October 7, 1915, reprinted in *Dunbar's Weekly*, n.d. (Hunt, vol. 18, 41). It seems a bit strange that since both Hunt and President Wilson were Democrats, the governor did not contact Wilson, inform him of the situation and request that he send no troops.

17 *Arizona Republican*, October 22, 1915.

18 *Ibid.*

19 *Ibid.*, October 23, 1915. In the 1914 elections, prohibition, an initiative measure, carried the state 25,887 to 22,743. In that total, 1,018 Greenlee County residents approved the action, while 1,031 were against it. (Report of the Secretary of State of Arizona, January 2, 1915, General Election Returns, 15.)

20 *Tucson Citizen*, October 5, 1915; R. L. Byrd, *El Paso Herald*, October 12, 1915 (Hunt, vol. 18, 43).

21 *Douglas Daily International*, October 20, 1915; *Arizona Republican*, October 5, 1915; *Tucson Citizen*, October 5, 1915.

22 *Copper Era*, October 8, 1915; *Tucson Citizen*, October 5, 1915; *Arizona Republican*, October 6, 1915.

23 *Arizona Republican*, October 12, 1915.

[24]*Ibid.*, October 17, 1915.

[25]*Ibid.*, October 21, 1915; *Arizona Daily Star*, October 21, 1915; *Copper Era*, October 22, 1915. Salarni had been one of the principal leaders in a 1903 strike in the district. He spent three years in the penitentiary as a result. At the start of the 1915 strike, he made speeches against the Western Federation, blaming that organization for his imprisonment. (*Arizona Republican*, October 19, 1915.)

[26] *Military Code of Arizona*, 15 July 1912, Section 59, 20 (General Order No. 11) in the Frank T. Alkire Collection, Arizona National Guard Box, APHS; *Arizona Daily Star*, August 26, 1915.

[27] Morris Goldwater of Maricopa County had introduced the repealing clauses. The general school fund, for example, had a $500,000 statutory appropriation which the legislators sought to cut to $100,000 annually. National Guard monies, likewise, were tied up because of this bill. (*Arizona Daily Star*, May 20, June 10, August 26, September 14, 1915.) In the case of the Clifton strike, the *Military Code of Arizona* provided that whenever the Guard was called out, the money to pay them was to come out of "any funds in the State Treasury, not otherwise appropriated." (Section 68, pp. 22–23.) The legislators' action banned Callaghan's use of such funds without their approval.

[28] *Arizona Gazette*, October 14, 1915 (Hunt, vol. 18, 53); *Tucson Citizen*, October 9, 1915; *Arizona Republican*, November 3, 1915.

[29] *El Paso Herald*, n.d. (Hunt, vol. 18, 52). In his scrapbook, the governor wrote on the edge of this article, "Arizona's Shame from the *El Paso Herald*, all tarred with the same stick. A paper that is owned by the same interest that owns the *Star, Bisbee Review, Douglas International Gazette, Copper Era*." *Pueblo Tribune* quoted in *Arizona Daily Star*, October 20, 1915. Colorado had experienced some of the bloodiest strikes in labor history as the result of the importation of strikebreakers, so perhaps Hunt had studied his history after all.

[30] *Copper Era*, June 11, July 30, 1915; *Arizona Gazette*, October 3, 1915 (Hunt, vol. 18, 57); *Arizona Republican*, October 22, 1915. One writer noted with interest that the "very people who had made the air vocal with dire predictions of the disaster impending over Arizona if the Constitution carrying the recall feature should be adopted were the first to invoke it." (J. H. Upton, "Current Topics," *Port Orford* (Oregon) *Tribune*, February 23, 1916 [Hunt, vol. 19, 28].)

[31] *Arizona Republican*, October 28, 1915.

[32] *Ibid.*

[33] The petition would have required 13,739 signatures or 25 percent of the total cast for governor in the 1914 election. (*Arizona Daily Star*, October 24, 1915.)

[34] *Arizona Republican*, October 26, 28, 1915; *Tucson Citizen*, October 29, 1915.

[35] "Clifton-Morenci Strike, 1915–1916"; *Denver Labor*, November 27, 1915 (Hunt, vol. 18, 107); *New Republic*, January 22, 1916, 306. On March 10, 1916, Creighton pleaded guilty in federal court to a charge of securing the publication of advertisements without having them marked as such in connection with this affair. (*Arizona Republican*, March 11, 1916.) Creighton was the only one prosecuted.

[36] *Arizona Republican*, October 20, 1915; *Copper Era*, October 29, 1915.

[37] *Arizona Republican*, October 28, 1915; *Arizona Gazette*, October 26, 1915 (Hunt, vol. 18, 30); *Copper Era*, November 5, 1915.

[38] *Arizona Republican*, November 9, 13, 1915.

[39] *Douglas Daily International*, November 30, 1915. The guardsmen finally were paid after the Arizona Supreme Court settled the case over the appropriations bill on December 23. (*Arizona Republican*, December 23, 1915.)

[40] *Arizona Daily Star*, November 14, 1915.

CHAPTER 4

[1] *Arizona Republican*, October 5, 1915. On October 7 the Greenlee County attorney appeared before Judge McWilliams and asked that the complaint against the managers be dismissed. The request was granted. (*Copper Era*, October 8, 1915.)

[2] *Dunbar's Weekly*, n.d. (Hunt, vol. 18, 41). The editor of the *Tucson Citizen* cited this as an example of Hunt's "economy." For eight cents, he asserted, the governor could have mailed the letter and for ten cents more he could have had it registered. (*Tucson Citizen*, October 12, 1915.)

[3] Article in unknown newspaper (Hunt, vol. 18, 45).

[4] *Tucson Citizen*, October 9, 1915.

[5] *Arizona Republican*, October 11, 1915.

[6] *Ibid.*

[7] *Tucson Citizen*, October 11, 1915.

[8] *Arizona Republican*, October 11, 1915.

[9] *Ibid.*, October 14, 1915; *Tucson Citizen*, October 15, 1915.

[10] *Arizona Republican*, October 19, 1915.

[11] *Ibid.*

[12] *Ibid.*, October 23, 1915.

[13] *Arizona Daily Star*, October 24, 1915.

[14] *Dunbar's Weekly*, n.d. (Hunt, vol. 18, 123); article in unknown newspaper (Hunt, vol. 18, 45); *Arizona Republican*, October 23, 1915.

[15] *Tucson Citizen*, October 23, 1915; *Arizona Republican*, October 24, 1915.

[16] *Arizona Republican*, October 24, 1915; *Copper Era*, October 29, 1915.

[17] *Arizona Republican*, October 25, 31, 1915.

[18] *Ibid.*, October 27, 1915.

[19] *Ibid.*, October 12, 1915; *Tucson Citizen*, October 22, 1915. Myers, the first commissioner of the Texas State Department of Labor, which he had helped organize, had a long career in industrial relations. (*Douglas Daily International*, October 31, 1915.)

[20] *Arizona Republican*, October 27, 1915. Davies was a former president of the Kentucky Coal Operators Association. This was his third appointment as a labor arbitrator in 16 months. He had acted in recent coal strikes in Colorado and Ohio. (*Copper Era*, November 12, 1915.)

[21] *Tucson Citizen*, October 7, 1915; *El Paso Herald*, October 9, 1915 (Hunt, vol. 18, 46).

[22] *Douglas Daily International*, October 6, 1915; *Arizona Republican*, October 24, 25, 1915.

[23] *Copper Era*, November 26, December 3, 1915.

[24] *Ibid.*, November 26, 1915; *Arizona Republican*, November 27, December 16, 1915.

[25] *Copper Era*, November 26, 1915; *Arizona Republican*, December 9, 1915. On December 22 Cash arranged with union leaders to permit the companies to resume operations, and the controversy ended. (*Copper Era*, December 24, 1915.)

[26] *Copper Era*, November 26, 1915; *Arizona Republican*, November 27, 1915.

[27] *Copper Era*, December 10, 1915.

[28] *Ibid.*, December 17, 31, 1915; *Arizona Republican*, December 12, 14, 18, 1915, January 1, 1916; *New Republic*, March 18, 1916, 186.

[29] *Copper Era*, December 17, 1915.

[30] *Arizona Republican*, December 11, 1915; *Arizona Daily Star*, December 21, 1915.

[31] *Arizona Republican*, December 19, 1915. One writer pointed out that this method of spending $100 per claim on assessments annually seemed to be a "proposal to cheat Uncle Sam." (*E&MJ*, January 22, 1916, 194.)

[32] *Arizona Daily Star*, December 25, 1915. E. H. Peplow, Jr., claimed that the strikers were holding out to prevent this work from being done in order to force a settlement on the managers. (Peplow, *History of Arizona* [New York: Lewis Historical Publishing Co., Inc., 1958], 2, 57.) On the contrary, the workers believed that by preventing the work, they were avoiding having a settlement forced on them.

[33] *Arizona Daily Star*, December 25, 1915; *Arizona Republican*, December 25, 1915. G. A. Franz, a prominent Clifton merchant, said that he would take the contract if he were not leaving for St. Louis the next day. Another businessman, Dell M. Potter, offered to do the work on 23 claims for $150 each, with $50 per claim going to the strikers' food fund. (*Tucson Citizen*, December 24, 1915.)

[34] *Copper Era*, December 24, 1915.

[35] *Ibid.*

[36] *Arizona Republican*, December 28, 1915. Sheriff Cash reported that a search of the men revealed 46 six-shooters, 1 Winchester rifle, and 12 dirks. (*Arizona Republican*, January 1, 1916.) Marshall Dillon denied that Cash ever searched the men, nor would he have had any right to do so. Dillon searched the assessors and took whatever weapons he found. (*Arizona Daily Star*, January 13, 1916.)

[37] *Copper Era*, December 31, 1915, January 14, 1916.

[38] *Ibid.*, December 31, 1915. The monthly average price of copper had risen steadily. In September it was 17.502¢; in October, 17.686¢; in November, 18.627¢; in December, 20.133¢. In January it jumped to 24.008¢ a pound. (*E&MJ*, September 1915 to February 1916.)

[39] *Copper Era*, December 31, 1915.

[40] *Arizona Republican*, January 2, 1916; *Daily Silver Belt*, January 10, 1916.

[41] *Daily Silver Belt*, January 7, 1916; *Copper Era*, January 7, 1916; *Arizona Republican*, January 7, 1916.

[42] *Arizona Republican*, January 15, 1916.

[43] Donnelly had worked for the Arizona Copper Company on the conveyor belts at the turn of the century. Later he moved to Miami, where he rose rapidly in the union organization. (*Copper Era*, January 14, 1916.) Donnelly was elected president of the Arizona State Federation of Labor in 1916.

[44] *Ibid.*; *Tucson Citizen*, January 14, 1916. The three locals were temporarily admitted to the Arizona State Federation, pending the approval of the American Federation of Labor. The idea of having the A.S.F.L. represent the strikers in negotiations was worked out in a conference between Donnelly and Dye. (*Daily Silver Belt*, January 7, 1916.)

[45] *Arizona Republican*, January 18, 1916.

[46] *Copper Era*, January 28, 1916; *Arizona Republican*, January 24, 1916. Financial assistance did not come as the strikers had hoped largely because the Clifton-Morenci workers had never supported organized labor in any other section. (*Daily Silver Belt*, January 26, 1916.)

CHAPTER 5

[1] *Copper Era*, January 21, February 4, 1916; *Arizona Republican*, January 18, 1916; *E&MJ*, February 5, 1916, 278.

[2] *Copper Era*, January 28, 1916; *Daily Silver Belt*, January 28, 1916.

[3] *Copper Era*, February 11, 1916; *Arizona Republican*, February 14, 1916.

[4] *Copper Era*, February 18, 25, 1916. The representatives of the workers included Theodore Hollingsworth (chairman), C. S. Edmondson (secretary), Dick Walsh, Rudolfo Palacios, Charles Duval, Encarnación Lucero, Francisco Maese, Pedro Mirelo, Lido Domínguez, Norberto Gonzales, Hilario Penas, Frank J. Starr, Fred W. Harris, José Bernal, Sam Bridges, Ignacio Aja, and Comito Vargas.

[5] Arizona Copper Company Payroll Records, 1915–16.

[6] *Copper Era*, March 31, 1916.

[7] *Arizona Labor Journal*, January 26, 1916; *E&MJ*, October 9, 1916, 606; Arizona Copper Company Payroll Records, 1916. Copper averaged 16.941¢ per pound in August 1915, the period from which the last pay before the strike was figured. The average price in February 1916, which determined the March wage rates, was 26.440¢ a pound, an increase of 9.499¢. (*E&MJ*, August 1915 to March 1916.)

[8] Copper sold for 12.75¢ a pound on January 2, 1915, and for 22.50¢ on December 31. The Shannon Company, whose only enterprise was its mine claims in the district, and hence the only one whose profits would accurately reflect conditions in Clifton-Morenci, reported net profits of $209,678 in 1915. *(E&MJ*, July 22, 1916, 185.) For the first six months of 1916 the company showed net earnings of $434,220. *(E&MJ*, September 30, 1916, 578.)

[9] *E&MJ*, August 26, 1916, 403.

[10] Norman Carmichael, *Some Factors Bearing on the Wage Question in the Clifton-Morenci-Metcalf District* (Clifton: July 1917), 6 (pamphlet in Arizona State Library and Archives, Phoenix).

[11] *Copper Era*, February 4, 1916; *Daily Silver Belt*, March 8, 1916. The final report of the executive committee showed total receipts of $24,174.13 and disbursements of $23,926 during the strike, plus the outstanding debt of $25,000. *(Copper Era*, February 4, 1916.)

[12] *Official Proceedings, Twenty-second Annual Convention*, Western Federation of Miners, Great Falls, Montana, 1916, 15–16; Jensen, *Heritage of Conflict*, 372–75.

[13] *Arizona Daily Star*, April 5, 1916; *Arizona Republican*, August 12, 1916.

[14] *Douglas Daily International*, December 22, 1915; *Arizona Daily Star*, April 4, 1916; *Arizona Republican*, August 25, September 5, 26, October 6, 1916; Effie R. Keen, "Arizona's Governors," *Arizona Historical Review*, October, 1930, 18; Richard E. Sloan and Ward R. Adams, *History of Arizona*, vol. 3 (Phoenix: Record Publishing Co., 1930), 74–77.

[15] "Autobiography of G. W. P. Hunt," typescript on microfilm, Arizona State Library and Archives, Phoenix, 166. The first part of Hunt's story was published in the *Arizona Historical Review* in January 1933. The official tabulation showed Hunt with 27,946 votes to Campbell's 29,976. Greenlee County gave 1,371 votes to Hunt and 968 to Campbell. *(Report of the Secretary of State of Arizona*, January 2, 1917.)

[16] *Copper Era*, December 15, 22, 1916.

[17] *Ibid.*, December 15, 1916; *Arizona Revised Statutes*, Section 2979.

[18] *The People Overruled*, pamphlet, n.p., n.d., Arizona State Library and Archives, 3; "The Autobiography of G. W. P. Hunt," 172. Campbell ran for the governorship again in 1918, won, and was reelected in 1920. The 1922 race saw Campbell versus Hunt, who was back on the stump after a four-year retirement. Once again Hunt beat Campbell.

[19] *Copper Era*, February 4, 1916; *Daily Silver Belt*, February 1, 1916.

[20] Letter to Governor Hunt, February 10, 1916 in "Clifton-Morenci Strike, 1915–16."

[21] *Tucson Citizen*, October 15, 1915; *Arizona Republican*, October 23, 1915; *New Republic*, March 18, 1916, 185.

Bibliography

The research for this study was done primarily in Tucson in the Special Collections Division of the University of Arizona Library and the Arizona Pioneers' Historical Society, and in Phoenix in the Arizona State Library and Archives.

Most useful among the unpublished materials were the Arizona Copper Company Payroll Records and a collection labeled "Clifton-Morenci Strike, 1915–1916," both at the University of Arizona. The former clears up many conflicting claims on wages and deductions, while the latter, though slim, offers much additional information. Of Governor Hunt's 70 volumes of scrapbooks, only volumes 18 and 19 pertain to this period. They contain mostly press clippings, many of which are not identified. Hunt's "autobiography" at the Arizona State Archives has little information on the strike, and his diaries at Arizona State University are disappointing. Two University of Arizona master's theses, Roberta Watt's "History of Morenci" and James Monroe Patton's "History of Clifton," are very useful for both background and bibliography.

Press coverage of the strike was extensive. The two best sources are the Phoenix *Arizona Republican,* which had a reporter in the district during most of the strike, and the *Copper Era,* a weekly newspaper published in Clifton. Tucson's *Arizona Daily Star* and the *Tucson Citizen* also gave the walkout full coverage, as did the extremely hostile Phoenix *Arizona Gazette.* The Miami *Daily Silver Belt* is good for a mining district's view of the events in Clifton-Morenci, while Governor Hunt's scrapbooks provide the main source for out-of-state reactions. The *Engineering and Mining Journal* is indispensible for information about the copper industry during the period.

Published materials that relate to the strike are scarce. The general histories, such as Arthur S. Link's *Woodrow Wilson and the Progressive Era,* are helpful for a general perspective of the times. The same is true of labor histories, such as Joseph G. Rayback's *History of American Labor,* Foster Rhea Dulles's *Labor in America,* and John R. Commons's *History of American Labour.* Vernon H. Jensen's *Heritage of Conflict,* a history of the Western Federation of Miners, is really the only book of direct relevance to this study. James B. Allen's *The Company Town in the American West* is suggestive. There is no good, comprehensive work on twentieth-century Arizona, and Governor Hunt deserves a good biography.

UNPUBLISHED MATERIALS

Arizona Copper Company Payroll Records, 1914–16. Special Collections, University of Arizona Library, Tucson.

"Autobiography of G. W. P. Hunt." Typescript on microfilm, Arizona State Library and Archives, Phoenix.

"Clifton-Morenci Strike, 1915–16." A collection of letters, statements, and articles on the strike. Special Collections, University of Arizona Library, Tucson.

Death Notices of Adjutant Generals, General Order 16, 5 August, 1949. National Guard of Arizona File, Arizona Pioneers' Historical Society, Tucson.

Diaries of Governor G. W. P. Hunt, 1915–17. Arizona State University Library, Tempe.

JOHNSON, ALAN V. "Governor G. W. P. Hunt and Organized Labor." Master's thesis, University of Arizona, 1964.

McGINNIS, TRU ANTHONY. "The Influence of Organized Labor on the Making of the Arizona Constitution." Master's thesis, University of Arizona, 1930.

Military Code of Arizona, General Orders 11, 15 July 1912. Frank T. Alkire Collection, Arizona National Guard Box, Arizona Pioneers' Historical Society, Tucson.

PATTON, JAMES MONROE. "The History of Clifton." Master's thesis, University of Arizona, 1945.

Reports of the Secretary of State of Arizona, 1915–17. Special Collections, University of Arizona Library, Tucson.

Scrapbooks of Governor G. W. P. Hunt, vols. 18 and 19. Special Collections, University of Arizona Library, Tucson.
WATT, ROBERTA. "The History of Morenci." Master's thesis, University of Arizona, 1956.

BOOKS AND PAMPHLETS

ALLEN, JAMES B. *The Company Town in the American West.* Norman: University of Oklahoma Press, 1966.
BRISSENDEN, PAUL F. *The I.W.W.* New York: Columbia University Press, 1920.
CARMICHAEL, NORMAN. *Some Factors Bearing on the Wage Question in the Clifton-Morenci-Metcalf District.* Clifton: n.p., July 1917. Pamphlet, Arizona State Library and Archives, Phoenix.
CLELAND, ROBERT GLASS. *History of Phelps Dodge, 1934–1950.* New York: Alfred A. Knopf, 1952.
COMMONS, JOHN R., DAVID J. SAPOSS, HELEN L. SUMNER, E. B. MITTELMAN, H. E. HOAGLAND, J. B. ANDREWS, AND SELIG PERLMAN. *History of Labour in the United States.* 4 vols. New York: Macmillan, 1918–35.
DONNELLY, THOMAS C., ed. *Rocky Mountain Politics.* Albuquerque: University of New Mexico Press, 1940.
DULLES, FOSTER RHEA. *Labor in America.* New York: Crowell, 1949.
JENSEN, VERNON H. *Heritage of Conflict.* Ithaca: Cornell University Press, 1950.
LINK, ARTHUR S. *Woodrow Wilson and the Progressive Era, 1910–1917.* New York: Harper & Row, 1954.
LOCKWOOD, FRANK C. *Arizona Characters.* Los Angeles: Times Mirror Press, 1928.
McCLINTOCK, JAMES H. *Arizona, the Youngest State,* vol. 2. Chicago: S. J. Clarke Publishing Co., 1916.
The People Overruled. n.d., n.p. Pamphlet, Arizona State Library and Archives, Phoenix.
PEPLOW, EDWARD H., JR. *History of Arizona.* New York: Lewis Historical Publishing Co., Inc., 1958.
RAYBACK, JOSEPH G. *A History of American Labor.* New York: The Free Press (Macmillan), 1951.
SLOAN, RICHARD E., AND WARD R. ADAMS. *History of Arizona,* vol. 3. Phoenix: Record Publishing Co., 1930.
WEED, W. H. *The Mines Handbook and Copper Handbook, 1916.* New York: n.p., 1916.
Western Federation of Miners. *Official Proceedings Twenty-second Annual Convention.* Great Falls, Montana: n.p., 1916.

NEWSPAPERS AND MAGAZINES, GENERAL REFERENCES

Arizona Daily Star (Tucson), 1915–16.
Arizona Gazette (Phoenix), 1915–16.
Arizona Republican (Phoenix), 1915–17.

Bisbee Daily Review, 1915–16.
Copper Era (Clifton), 1914–16.
Daily Silver Belt (Miami), 1915–16.
Douglas Daily International, 1915–16.
Engineering and Mining Journal, 1914–16.
Tucson Citizen, 1915–16.

NEWSPAPERS AND MAGAZINES, SPECIFIC REFERENCES

DOUGLAS, WALTER, Letter to the Editor. *The New Republic* 6 (March 18, 1916): 185–87.
FITCH, JOHN A. "Arizona's Embargo on Strike-Breakers." *The Survey* 36 (May 6, 1916): 143–46.
"Greenlee's Mines and Farms." *Arizona, the State Magazine* 5 (November 1914): 14–27.
HUNT, GEORGE W. P. Letter to the Editor. *The New Republic* 6 (April 15, 1916): 293.
KARTUS, SIDNEY. "The Autobiography of George Wiley Paul Hunt." *Arizona Historical Review* 5 (January 1933): 253–63.
KEEN, EFFIE R. "Arizona's Governors." *Arizona Historical Review* 3 (October 1930): 7–20.
MACFARLANE, PETER CLARK. "The Galahad of Arizona: Governor Hunt." *Collier's* 57 (April 15, 1916): 21–27.
PATTEE, SAMUEL L. "Governor Hunt — A Personal Appreciation." *Arizona Historical Review* 6 (April 1935): 44–48.
"A Strike Without Disorder." *The New Republic* 5 (January 22, 1916): 304–6.

Many other newspaper and magazine articles concerning the strike are contained in Governor Hunt's scrapbooks, Special Collections, University of Arizona, Tucson. Some of these articles are unlabeled or untitled, and bibliographic information cannot be complete. Labeled sources include the following:

Arizona Labor Journal, January 26, 1916.
Denver Labor, November 27, 1915.
Des Moines News (Iowa), January 10, 1915.
Dunbar's Weekly, n.d.
El Paso Herald, October 12, 1915, and n.d.
Mining and Scientific Press, November 11, 1915.
Mining Journal (Clifton), May 30, 1929.
New York Call, November 7, 1915.
Port Orford (Oregon) *Tribune,* February 23, 1916.

Index